BASEBALL Letters

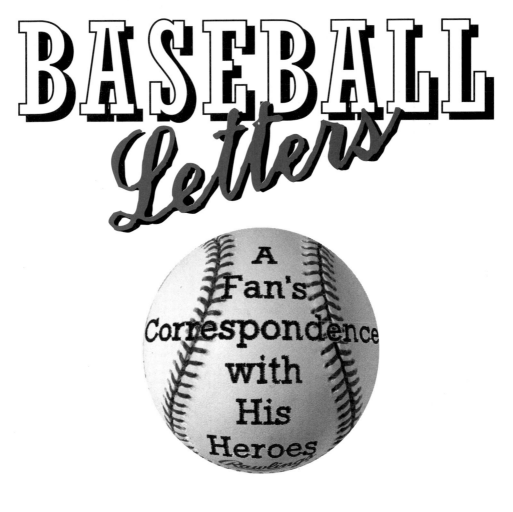

A Fan's Correspondence with His Heroes

Seth Swirsky

Designed by Steven Brower

KODANSHA INTERNATIONAL
New York • Tokyo • London

Kodansha America, Inc.

114 Fifth Avenue, New York, New York 10011, U.S.A.

Kodansha International Ltd.

17-14 Otowa 1-chome, Bunkyo-ku, Tokyo 112, Japan

Published in 1996 by Kodansha America, Inc.

ISBN   1-56836-152-1

LC   96-77706

Printed in the United States of America

96 97 98 99 00   RRD/H   10 9 8 7 6 5 4 3 2 1

Dedicated to my father and my son

Contents

"Many times I've had the thoughts "a beautiful day, this is amazing. . . . "
—Claude Osteen

Preface

In the summer of 1994 two important events occurred in my life. My first child, Julian, was born and the baseball players went on strike. While I was becoming happily accustomed to my growing family, I was also missing the sounds of baseball in my home. I decided I'd keep in touch with the game by writing to a few former players. When I started getting some great responses back, I kept on sending letters. It became a daily thing, writing to more players and running to the mailbox to see who had replied. If you're a baseball fan, you can imagine what it felt like to open a letter from Al Kaline or Ted Williams. This experience reminded me of when, as a boy, I wrote to my favorite players and waited eagerly for each day's mail to see if any of my heroes had sent me their autograph.

The personally handwritten letters I received were wonderful—full of great stories, colorful anecdotes, heartfelt sentiments, and lessons about life. As weeks and then months passed, and my baseball letters grew from a dozen to the hundreds, I knew that the enthusiastic reactions of my close friends could not be exceptional. Everyone, I thought, from baseball purists to casual observers, would love to peek into the players' own thoughts about historic events that shaped their lives and the lives of their fans.

On the following pages of *Baseball Letters* are the questions I asked each player—the famous and not so famous—and his own words in his own handwriting.

Because most players responded on the same page on which my letter was written, their answers complete a kind of intimate conversation. It is my hope that these responses will allow the reader to "see," as I did, how the player felt as he mulled over the question and then committed his answer to the page. When Duke Snider wrote about what it meant for the Dodgers to finally beat the Yankees, he made the event come alive for me in a way that was much more powerful than any account in a standard baseball history book. I hope his answer does the same for you. Like the Duke, the other players used only limited space, so their answers go right to the point.

Some players, wanting to explain their answers further, even called me! I was in the middle of writing a song when Cleveland Indian great Bob Feller called. So did former Yankee great Jerry Coleman. One late summer evening, Roy Partee, catcher for the '46 Red Sox, called to describe, in vivid detail, Enos Slaughter's famous "Mad Dash" to score the winning run of the World Series for the St. Louis Cardinals. As he talked about this thrilling play, I got a real "feel" for what had happened that day— maybe Johnny Pesky didn't hesitate as much as the history books say he did!

Everyday, my routine was hostage to the whim of my letter carrier's schedule. Would Cal Ripken, Jr., write back? How about Harmon Killebrew? Leo Nonnenkamp? I got so accustomed to receiving these fabulous letters—seven a day during a one-month stretch—that when they didn't arrive, I was decidedly downcast.

There is something about baseball that captures and forever encapsulates the purity and unquestioning belief of one's youth. Writing to someone who played the game when I was growing up—anyone who played for the '69 Mets, for instance—immediately transports me back to that idyllic summer and autumn.

These letters compel my imagination to go to work, as when I listen to a great baseball game on the radio. When Whitey Ford, for example, wrote to me about going to Yankee Stadium as a ten-year-old to watch his hero, Joe DiMaggio, I could easily visualize it because it taps into the same feeling I had for my heroes.

Many people have told me that putting this book together was a "good idea." In truth, I wrote the letters initially because I wanted answers to many questions that have intrigued me. And the players answered me, I believe, because they enjoyed recalling the event, setting the record straight, or just plain reminiscing. It was the enjoyment of reading the letters and sharing them with my family and friends that finally gave me the idea to share the wealth of these wonderful stories with as many people as possible.

When re-reading these letters, as I often do, and reflecting on their meaning, I realize that baseball is ultimately not about winning or losing, but about living. In the results-oriented world in which we live, it is easy to lose sight of the process and of the "real life" people who are involved in both the business and the joy of baseball.

Yes, the big home run is the stuff of memory. But what surrounded that home run, or that slide, or that missed opportunity—that is the real drama, often thrilling, sometimes poignant, occasionally tragic.

The players I met through these baseball letters were, in a very tangible way, voices from the past. Seeing their handwriting, speaking to them on the phone, learning their insights—all of it gave me a greater understanding, not only of baseball's past, but of America's.

Before some of the players signed releases for their letters to be reprinted, they asked me to make it clear that they were simply expressing their opinions. That request has been honored. All the letters are reprinted here as they were written by me and the players—mistakes, misspellings, and all. Additionally, a portion of the proceeds from this book will be donated to the Baseball Assistance Team (BAT), an organization devoted to helping former major league players who are in financial need.

Baseball Letters is dedicated to my father and son, my two favorite guys. Every time I received a new baseball letter, I would fax it to my dad and we would bat such questions back and forth as, "Did Babe Ruth really call his shot in the 1932 World Series?" and "Should Bill Buckner have been removed in the late innings of Game 6 in the 1986 Series?" I would also show my little boy the letters and say things like, "Someday, I'll tell you how great this guy was." But that's in his future. For now, I will simply ask you to get comfortable in your favorite chair and enjoy these baseball letters.

May 1996

WOODY ENGLISH
Born 1907, Fredonia, Ohio.
Shortstop, third baseman,
1927–1938; Chicago Cubs
(team captain) and Brooklyn
Dodgers. In game three of the
1932 Yankees–Cubs World Series,
Babe Ruth supposedly pointed
out to center field and then hit
Cubs pitcher Charlie Root's next
pitch over the center field wall
for a home run. Thus, the legend
of the "Called Shot."

(Inset) Babe at bat, moments
before his historic home run.

November Nights Music Inc.

January 17, 1995

Dear Mr. English:

I am a 34 year-old songwriter living in Los Angeles. I know your time is very valuable, but I wondered if you could tell me (below) if Ruth called his shot in the '32 Series? Also, did the blast quiet down the Cub bench? I truly would be fascinated to know sir.

I've enclosed a self-addressed, stamped envelope for your convenience if you decide to jot down a note or two. Again, thank you so much for your time.

Sincerely,

Seth Swirsky

Seth Swirsky

Seth- Babe Ruth did not call his H.R. I was playing 3rd Base that game and he held two fingers up indicating two strikes - The press indicated he pointed which he did not - He never said he called it. When asked he replyed the papers said I did

The Cub bench never let up on him -

Woody English

3

Cal Ripken, Jr., Cal Ripken, Sr.

CAL RIPKEN, JR.

Born 1960, Havre de Grace, Maryland. Shortstop, 1981–present; Baltimore Orioles. Since June 5, 1982, he has literally been the Orioles' everyday shortstop, succeeding in 1995 in breaking Lou Gehrig's longstanding record of 2130 consecutive games played. He has more home runs than any shortstop in history (327 and still mounting) and was the 1982 Rookie of the Year and 1983 and 1991 American League MVP. Many of our fathers taught us how to play baseball. I wondered how this great athlete learned the game from his dad, a onetime O's manager.

Dec. 21, 1995

Dear Seth,

When I was small, I remember competing with my sister and brothers for time with my dad. Baseball occupied a lot of my dad's time, but he spent as much time as he could with us kids.

On Saturday mornings, my dad conducted a baseball clinic for the Orioles. I quickly figured out that because my sister and my brothers weren't interested in a boring baseball clinic, I could go with my dad and get some time alone with him.

The hours in the car spent with my dad driving to and from the ballpark on Saturday mornings still remains one of my most vivid — and favorite - childhood memories.

Sincerely,

Cal

5

	1	2	3	4	5	6	7	8	9	10	R	H
B.KLYN.	0	0	0	0	0	0	0	0	0		0	0
YANKS	0	0	0	1	0	1	0	0			2	5

DON LARSEN
Born 1929, Michigan City, Indiana. Righthanded pitcher, 1953–1965, 1967; N.Y. Yankees and seven other teams. On the day he was served with divorce papers, he pitched the only perfect game in World Series history, October 8, 1956, for the Yankees (against the Brooklyn Dodgers). It was the first perfect game pitched in the majors since 1922. In 1959 the Yankees traded him for a guy named Roger Maris.

AT BAT 8 POS
BALL 1 STRIKE 2

December 27, 1994

Dear Mr. Larsen:

I am a 34 year-old songwriter living in Los Angeles. I
have read many accounts of your no-hitter in the '56
Series. But in none of them do they say at what point
in the contest you actually began thinking that it
might be attainable or whether you were nervous in the
ninth.

EVERY PITCHER KNOWS WHEN THE FIRST
HIT HAPPENS. I FIGURED THERE WAS A CHANCE
AFTER THE 7TH INNING BUT FACING THE DODGERS
OF THAT ERA YOU KNEW THAT ANYTHING COULD
HAPPEN.
    I WAS VERY NERVOUS IN THE 9TH BUT CONSCIOUS
OF THE FACT THAT THIS WAS A BIG GAME AND
THAT I HAD EIGHT GREAT PLAYERS BEHIND ME

August 7, 1995

Dear Mr. Cain:

I am a 35 year-old songwriter living in Los Angeles. I love studying baseball history and I recently read that you were the pitcher who pitched to the midget Eddie Gaedel. I know your time is very valuable sir, but I wondered if you could tell me (below) if you talked to your batterymate Bob Swift about how to pitch Gaedel? Were you shocked to see him step to the plate or did you know that Gaedel would bat that day? I would be truly fascinated by your response sir if you decide to jot down a note or two. Again, thank you for your time.

Very Sincerely,

Seth Swirsky

Seth Swirsky

BOB CAIN

Born 1924, Longford, Kansas. Righthanded pitcher, 1949–1953; Chicago White Sox, Detroit Tigers, and St. Louis Browns. On August 19, 1951, Bill Veeck, the Barnumesque St. Louis Browns' owner, sent a three-foot, seven-inch man named Eddie Gaedel to the plate for what would be his only major league at-bat, in baseball's most famous stunt. Cain walked him on four pitches.

Bob Swift and I did talk about pitching to Eddie and Bob wanted to lay down to give me a low target, but Ed Husley, the umpire, said no. None of us knew anything about Eddie coming to bat. The main thing is that we won the game 6-2.

Bob Cain

Dear Seth:

In response to your letter, I am writing my recollection of the play that involved Jackie Robinson and me.

I can see the play just as clear as when it happened. It was a low throw and Jackie pulled his foot off the bag. When he placed it back, his foot was in the middle of the base. I had no recourse but to unintentionally step on his ankle. As I have always contended this was not a deliberate action. Ken Burns made the remark that I "sliced his thigh open" but there was no blood what so ever. I do not know where he finds his sources, but I wish he would share them with me! Burns continually hangs up on me when I have called him to question him about these falsehoods.

Recently on an ESPN documentary on baseball a remark made by Rex Barney said that Jackie retaliated for the first base incident by knocking out all of my teeth when I slid into second base. What a joke! People can fabricate more and more nonsense about this play but I know the truth because I was there!

I love the game of baseball and played every game with all of my heart. I am sorry this incident has caused so much controversy . I know the truth and that is I never intentionally spiked Jackie Robinson.

Sincerely yours,

Enos Slaughter

Jackie Robinson

ENOS SLAUGHTER
Born 1916, Roxboro, North Carolina.
Outfielder, 1938–1942, 1946–1959;
mostly with the St. Louis Cardinals
and New York Yankees. Hall of
Fame, 1985. His aggressive style on
the basepaths won the 1946 World
Series as he scored on a single—
"Slaughter's Mad Dash"—the
deciding run of the Series. In 1947,
controversy surrounded him as he
slid, spikes high, right into the
rookie who was playing first base,
Jackie Robinson. I wanted to know
whether it was just "hard-nosed"
baseball or if he meant to send a
message to the first black player in
the majors.

1/4/96

Dear Mr. Swirsky,

I received your letter and thanks for the donation. Yes we had quite a few white fans at our games especially when we played in the major leagues parks.

No we never had any resentment toward the white teams. But there was one minor league team in Brooklyn that pulled some dirty tricks on us in order to beat us. They would freeze one set of balls over nite for us to hit and their white umpires gave us the regular balls to pitch to them. They could hit the balls out of the park, and we couldn't hit the frozen balls out of the infield. We never knew they were doing this until after our league folded.

Hope I answered your questions,

Yours Truly

Bill Peace

February 13, 1995

Dear Mr. Erskine:

I wondered if you could tell me what was the most nervous you ever were on the mound-- what was the situation?

2/26/95

Hi Seth -

The most nervous I ever was on a baseball field was Dodger Stadium - July 1992 when I played the Canadian + American National Anthems before a Montreal/Dodger game - on my harmonica. — 45,000 attendance (I really enjoy music) (no mistakes)

Actually I was always keyed up before I pitched but was truly never nervous. — As close as I ever came however, was my rookie year when I was called in to pitch in Pitts — bases loaded to face Ralph Kiner — The crowd was going crazy for Kiner to hit a grand slam — I did not disappoint that big Pitts. crowd. —

Regards - Carl Erskine

TED WILLIAMS
Born 1918, San Diego,
California. Outfielder,
1939–1942, 1946–1960;
Boston Red Sox. Hall of
Fame, 1966. Considered by
many to be the greatest
"pure" hitter who ever
played, he had 521 career
home runs, a .344 lifetime
average, six batting titles,
and won two MVP awards.
The only player to equal
his two Triple Crowns was
Rogers Hornsby.

September 13, 1995

Dear Mr. Williams:

I am a 35 year-old songwriter living in Los Angeles. I
think you, Lou Gehrig and Babe Ruth truly were the best
hitters the game has ever seen. I know your time is
very valuable sir, but I wondered if you could tell me
(below) if you ever learned anything about hitting
from watching or talking to either Mr. Ruth or Mr.
Gehrig? I would be fascinated by your response, if you
decide to jot down a note or two.

Thank you again for your time and have a nice day. You
were great.

With Much Respect,

Seth Swirsky

*Best advise was from
Rogers Hornsby
"get a good ball to hit"*

Ted Williams

CARROLL HARDY
Born 1933, Sturgis, South
Dakota. Outfielder, 1958–
1964, 1967; Boston Red Sox
and three other teams. He
has the unique distinction of
pinch-hitting for Roger Maris
(when Hardy hit his first
home run), Carl Yastrzemski,
and Ted Williams.

December 2, 1995

Dear Mr. Hardy:

I am a 35 year-old songwriter living in Los Angeles. I
enjoy reading baseball history and I read that you
were the only man to pinch-hit for the great Ted
Williams. That must have been something--do you
remember it?

In August 1960 Ted's last year, Ted fouled
a pitch off the foot. It hurt him so much
that he had to leave the game. I was called
to finish his at bat. No one thought a thing
about it at the time. It wasn't until Ted
finished the 1960 season and all his statistics
were finalized that they realized that the
time I finished his at bat was the only
time anyone ever pinch hit for Ted.

Carroll Hardy
The only man to pinch hit
for Ted Williams

15

Heavy hitters: Bill Terry, Ted Williams,
Rogers Hornsby, George Sisler

17

DAVE STAPLETON
Born 1954, Fairhope, Alabama. Infielder, 1980–1986; Boston Red Sox. He was brought in as Bill Buckner's defensive replacement at first base throughout the '86 season, but, to the surprise of many, he did not replace Buckner in the fateful 10th inning of game six of the 1986 World Series. When Mookie Wilson's dribbler skipped through the hobbled Buckner's legs, the stunned Boston faithful could only ask, "What if . . . ?"

. . . During . . .

. . . and After—Buckner's unfortunate boot

January 25, 1995

Dear Mr. Stapleton:

I am a 34 year old songwriter living in Los Angeles. I know your time is very valuable, but I wondered if you could tell me (below), if you were surprised that McNamara didn't put you in late in the 6th game of the '86 World Series replacing Buckner?

Matt,

Yes, I was surprised because I had already loosened up my legs and arm to go into the game in the 7th inning. I had usually gone in at this time in all other play-off games if we were ahead. The reason he left Buckner in was to be on the field when we won the game so he could celebrate with the others. As you well know, nobody got to celebrate because of this bad decision. Mr. McNamara never did have my respect as a manager or person but that doesn't matter. It does no good to beat a dead dog. He has to live with his decision the rest of his life. And great Red Sox fans all over the country have to continue to suffer on as a result of it. And I feel sometimes that, I got released after the "86" season because he didn't want me there to remind him of his mistake. I have talked to hundreds & hundreds of fans in the past years but none by mail. I hope this helps you understand.

Sincerely,
Dave Stapleton

19

JOHN McNAMARA
Born 1932, Sacramento, California.
Manager, 1969–1970, 1974–1977, 1979–
1988, 1990–1991, with six teams, 1150
wins. I asked this manager of the '86
Red Sox what made that team tick
and if he ever felt stung by those
who questioned his move not to
replace Buckner with Stapleton.

December 12, 1994

Dear Mr. McNamara:

I just wanted to tell you that I thought you made the right
decision in keeping Bill Buckner at first in the 6th game of the
'86 World Series. He was a 17 year veteran and a guy that
helped you get there. Leading by two runs in the top of the
tenth inning, he deserved to be out on the field. That was one
of the great comeback teams of all time and it's to bad you
couldn't have won it all.

I wondered if you could tell me what made that team click?

Sincerely,

Seth Swirsky

Seth:

    Sorry for the delay in returning your letter. I guess the answer to your question was 1ˢᵗ, Talent. We puts a team concept, as our priority, which I tried to do every place that I managed. It was fun & I tried to dismiss my media critics because they have never shared what I lived & enjoyed. Thank you for your kind message.

    Sincerely

    John McNamara

HARMON KILLEBREW
Born 1936, Payette, Idaho.
First and third baseman,
1954–1975; mostly with the
Washington Senators/
Minnesota Twins franchise.
Hall of Fame, 1984. The 1969
A.L. MVP, he hit 573 home
runs, fifth on the all-time list,
leading the league six times
and hitting over 40 home
runs in eight seasons. I wondered if his dad saw him hit
his 500th home run.

8-29-95

Dear Seth,

Please forgive the long delay in answering your letter! I even took it to Japan with me in hopes that I would get it answered!

In answer to your question about my father — he passed away when I was 16 and never got to see me play Major League baseball. But, he was the biggest influence on my athletic Career. He got me started playing all sports at a very early age. You may have heard my Hall of Fame acceptance speech when I told how my mother was complaining to my Dad about the holes in the yard and he told her we weren't raising grass — we're raising boys!

Sincerely,

Harmon Killebrew

23

PHIL NIEKRO
Born 1939, Blaine, Ohio. Righthanded pitcher, 1964–1987; mostly with the Milwaukee/Atlanta Braves. A knuckleball specialist, he won 318 games, pitching until he was 48. Amazingly, he won only 31 games before he was 30, and won 121 after the age of 40 (a record). Only Cy Young, Pud Galvin, and Walter Johnson pitched more innings than Niekro's 5403.1. Phil and his brother Joe won a combined total of 539 games, more than any other pitching pair of brothers.

November Nights Music Inc.

February 13, 1995

Dear Mr. Niekro:

I was always impressed with the relationship you and your brother had with your dad. I wondered, what was the greatest game you ever pitched in front of your dad?

Sincerely,

Seth Swirsky

Its a longer story than I can write on this paper. My greatest game for me was when I won my 300th game in 1985 while pitching with the Yankees, winning the game 1-0 while my father was on his death bed. It took me 5 games to finally win it, how he held on that long I will never know. Someday maybe I can tell you the whole story about it

It is truly a movie waiting to be put together (Hopefully)

Sincerly
Phil Niekro

December 21, 1994

Dear Mr. Camilli:

I wondered if you could tell me what baseball
was like in your day? Also, what was your favorite
team to play for!

DOLPH CAMILLI
Born 1907, San Francisco, California.
First baseman, 1933–1943, 1945; mostly
with the Brooklyn Dodgers and
Philadelphia Phillies. The 1941 National
League MVP hit 239 home runs in his
impressive career, belting 23 or more
for eight straight years, 1935–1942.

More fun and less money.
Brooklyn Dodgers
Dolph Camilli

AL GIONFRIDDO
Born 1922, Dysart, Pennsylvania. Outfielder, 1944–1947; Pittsburgh Pirates and the Brooklyn Dodgers. Made one of the World Series' most memorable catches when he snared Joe Dimaggio's 415-foot drive in the sixth inning of the sixth game of the 1947 World Series, preserving the win for Brooklyn.

December 23, 1994

Dear Mr. Gionfriddo:

I wonder if you could tell me what it was like to play
baseball in the 1940's. It seems like such an idyllic time.

It was great to play in the 40's
we did not make much money but
we play hard because it was a job
and we play for our fans. They
knew all the players by first names.
Al Gionfriddo

BOBBY THOMSON
Born 1923, Glasgow, Scotland.
Outfielder/third baseman,
1946–1960; mostly with the
New York Giants and Milwaukee
Braves. The "Staten Island Scot"
hit 264 home runs, the most
important being the dramatic
"Shot Heard 'round the World."
That three-run homer in the bot-
tom of the ninth inning on
October 3, 1951 wrested the pen-
nant from the devastated
Brooklyn Dodgers, who had been
way ahead of the Giants most
of that summer.

January 3, 1995

Dear Mr. Thomson:

I am a 34 year-old songwriter living in Los Angeles. I
know your time is very valuable, but I wondered if you
could tell me (below or on back) who your baseball
heroes were growing up and whether you ever got a
chance to play with/against them? Also, do you ever
watch that clip of your famous home run when you're by
yourself?

Hello Seth, nice to hear from you.
I admired Joe Di Maggio because he played the game with
dignity and grace. I admired Ted Williams for his
batting prowess. I played against Joe in the 1951 series
and I played with Ted at Boston in 1960.
I have been by myself a few times in my life
when the Home run was shown. It's a bit of a thrill by myself
more so than when I'm with a group.

Best Regards,
Bobby Thomson

1/26/95

Dear Seth.

Received your letter in regards to Bobby Thomson's "Shot heard around the world". At first I thought I would have a chance at it because it was a line drive. But instead of a sinking line drive, it took off. It would be an out in Ebetts Field but the Polo Grounds it was a home run!

To me it was one of the biggest disappointments of my major league career. A few years later I am a member of the Braves when Thomson is traded to the Braves, and now we are team mates.

Not only did he become a
team mate but my room mate.
I asked him how he felt
after he hit the famous
home run and his answer
was thats history, did
not want to talk about it.
He showed me a lot of class.
To this day - I tell
people - if anyone hit that
home run, I am glad it
was Bobby Thomson.
At least I am part of
history - watching the
home run with me watching
it go over my head.
I am often asked about it.
But at the time it was a
big big disappointment.

Regards -

Andy Pafko -

33

Mickey Mantle

August 15, 1995

Dear Mr. Johnson:

I loved Mickey Mantle and I read once how you had
something to do with him getting the # 7. Is that true?
I would truly be thrilled if you could tell me how the
Mick got his number and why he coveted it so.

*at the start of the 51 season
I had # 7 and Micky wanted that # 7
badly. I said OK it didn't make any differen
to me so I took # 24 thats all that
was to it.*

Bill

35

Dear Seth,

In response to your inquiry as to my favorite player growing up and an incident with them, must admit I had 2. During my youth, and up until I saw Ken Griffey Jr. play, I will tell you Willie Mays is the best all-around player I ever saw. I grew up in the South Bronx, and equally idolized Willie and Mickey Mantle (if he only had healthy legs). Two different styles of player, but both great.

Mickey Mantle, was a myth, not a real person. In the early 50's, we did not have a TV, only baseball cards, and stories from the rich kids who had TV. When I did see him on TV, he was god-like the way he went into his home run trot, the way he stood at home plate, his swing. I had an All-American look, and an aura about him. As every other kid did, I tried running like him.

I had played stickball with my brother Bob, in the late 40's, before I had seen Mantle switc hit, and I was switch hitting only to protect myself from my nine-year-old brother's erratic pitching. We also played "lefty-only" baseball. When there were only a few kids to play we would only make the right side of the field fair ball, the left side foul, so the few could cover t playing surface— thus, I had to hit left-handed. This of course, leading up to actually seeing Mantle on TV switch hit, and feeling a bonding with him, and fantasizing, me being him each time he came to the plate.

When I moved to Jersey, and played Little League, and switch hit, I was referred to as tryi to act like Mickey, but in actuality my Little League coach, a woman named Janet Murk (she was the ex-second baseman for our high school team and a switch hitter), convinced me to continue switch hitting.

I don't remember what year it was, but it was at the end of Mickey's career, we went into New York for a series with the Yankees. Mickey played first base, and I had just been intentio ally walked to load the bases. Mickey played behind me, my run meaning nothing. Lefty Stev Barber was on the mound. He went into his stretch, to avoid a squeeze, and looked over at m at first. I was staring at him right in the face, knowing if his hands were below his belt, he wa coming to first and if his hands were by his uniform letters, he was going home (most lefties can't help it). Besides Steve staring at me, so was my father, step-mother, brothers, sisters, aunts, uncles and every relative I had left tickets for that day, 55 in all, a new American Leagu record. I felt a thump on my back, and heard Mickey's familiar voice say, "Sorry Richie." I wa staring at Steve Barber and mentally picturing Mickey Mantle and those huge forearms, and never noticed Barber throwing over to first. I only had a 3 foot lead.

In 1965, my first spring training, we played the Giants at Hy Corbett Field in Tucson. Mays lifted a lazy fly ball to me in right. I caught it for the second out, and put it in my back et The umpires came out to get the ball from me, and I would not give it up. He was my favorite player. They finally succumbed to my wishes and entered a new ball into the game, and som where in my baseball collection, I have a ball hit by Willie Mays, that I caught down by my be just where Willie would have caught it if I hit a lazy fly ball to him. One of my 2 favorite base players.

I PLAYED AND INTERACTED WITH MY 2 FAVORITE PLAYERS OF ALL TIME, EVERY KID'S DREAM.

In one moment in time, it is nice to have your name linked to a soul of history, the late Micl Mantle.

Richie Scheinblum

Richie Scheinblum 10/31/95

Pine-tarred and feathered

TIM McCLELLAND
Born 1951, Jackson, Mississippi. Umpire who was behind the plate during the "pine tar" game. On July 24, 1983, he ruled that George Brett—who had just given his Royals the lead with a towering ninth-inning home run—had swabbed pine tar too far up on the barrel of his bat, thus nullifying his blast. American League President Lee MacPhail overturned the decision and ordered a resumption of the game, which the Royals won, 5-4.

August 14, 1995

Dear Mr. McClelland:

I remember the infamous "pine tar" game where you were the home plate umpire. I will never forget George Brett coming at you from the dugout when you called him out after he hit that mammoth home run off of Gossage. It looked like he was going to come right through the television!

I wondered if you could tell me (below) if you were a little nervous for your safety, at the time, when he charged you? Also, was it a tough call to make at the time?

Seth,
    I wasn't scared because Brett was charging out at a man who stands 6'6" tall, weighs 250 pounds, had protective equipment on, and had a bat in his hand — George wasn't very smart! We are happy with our call because we went by the rule book and called what we had to do.
    Thanks for writing. It is nice to hear from people concerning umpiring.

Sincerely,
Tim McClelland
A.L. #36

January 20, 1995

Dear Mr. Brett:

Your brother was one of my favorite players growing up. I've
noticed that in many interviews he has given, he always brings
your name up. I wondered if you could tell me when you first
knew that George was a special hitter?   Also, were you more
successful against him in the majors or your backyard growing up?

I was 17 when learning to play pro ball. George
was 12. Hard for me to notice his ability. My
father always thought he would be the better hitter.
When he reached the majors - we were in opposite
leagues.... I never saw him play... but friends told
me he was going to be special.

He hit about 300 off me career wise. and I
wanted to beat him very bad -

KB

39

Dear Mr. Ferrell:

I am a 34 year-old songwriter living in Los Angeles. I know your time is very valuable but I wondered if you could tell me (below) who were the best pitchers you caught and who were the pitchers that you wish you had caught during your fabulous career? I would truly be interested in your response sir.

Again, I thank you very much for your time. I've enclosed a self-addressed, stamped envelope for your convenience.

Very Sincerely,

Seth Swirsky

I have been asked that question many times — I always answer by saying —
The greatest left hand pitcher I ever caught was Lefty Grove
The greatest right hander I ever caught was my brother Wes Ferrell
Rick Ferrell

40

CK FERRELL (right)
rn 1905, Durham, North
rolina. Died 1995. A Hall
Fame catcher, he played
r 18 years (1929-1947),
ostly with the St. Louis
owns, Boston Red Sox,
d Washington Senators.
ly 4 players caught more
mes than he did.

s brother Wes Ferrell, a
ssible future Hall-of-
mer, was the best hitting
cher ever. He holds the
cord for the most career
me runs by a pitcher (38)
d the most home runs by
pitcher in a single season
th 9 (1931). They played
gether on the Red Sox
d Senators from 1934 to
38 and are the best
own brother-battery in
jor league history.

February 18, 1995

DEAR MR. SWIRSKY,

In reference to your letter inquiring of my friendship with HENRY AARON prior to, and after April 8th, 1974, I find that to be the most interesting question I've been asked relative to that event. I knew Mr. AARON only as a fellow Major League Baseball player, both before, and after, the event, and contrary to media reporting, most Professional Athletes are ACQUAINTANCES, involved in the same field of endeavor, not "soul buddies", as is often depicted.

Best Always,

Al Downing

AL DOWNING
Born 1941, Trenton, N.J. Lefthanded pitcher, 1961–1977; mostly with the New York Yankees and Los Angeles Dodgers. A career 123-game winner, he will always be remembered for giving up Hank Aaron's 715th home run, on April 8th, 1974, the shot that broke Babe Ruth's all-time record. I wondered if he was friends with Aaron before that historic hit and if it changed their relationship.

DUKE SNIDER

Born 1926, Los Angeles, California. Centerfielder, 1947–1964; mostly with the Brooklyn/Los Angeles Dodgers. Hall of Fame, 1980. The all-time Dodger leader in home runs with 389, he hit 407 all told, including the most home runs in the major leagues in the decade of the 1950s—326. He played in 36 games in six World Series, all against the Yankees, hitting 11 home runs, the fourth-highest total. He was a member of great Brooklyn clubs that lost the Series to the Yankees in '47, '49, '52, '53, and '56. But not in 1955!

January 9, 1995

Dear Mr. Snider:

Although you played a little before my time, I have always had an
affinity for the '55 Dodgers. I even have a baseball signed by the
whole team!

I wondered if you could tell me what it meant for you personally,
to finally beat the Yankees in the '55 Series?

IT PROVED TO ALL FANS AND TO
US THAT WE WERE AS GOOD OF
A TEAM AS THE YANKEES NOT
BETTER BUT AS GOOD!

Duke

JOHNNY PODRES
Born 1932, Witherbee, New York. Lefthanded pitcher, 1953–1955, 1957–1967, 1969; mostly with the Brooklyn/Los Angeles Dodgers. He rode his great change-up to a record of 148 wins and 116 losses (four wins and one loss in World Series play). He will always be remembered as the guy who pitched the Brooklyn Dodgers to their first World Championship, shutting out the Yankees, 2-0, in game seven on October 4, 1955.

Amoros's mom

December 15, 1994

Dear Mr. Podres:

I've always had an affinity for the '55' Brooklyn Dodgers.
I wondered if you could tell me a little about that team --
what really made it go?

Best Wishes
Johnny Podres

The Dodgers of 55 had many veteran
players who knew how to play,
they were embarrassed by the Yankees many
times and I as a young pitcher was very
thrilled to be a Dodger and thanks to Sandy
Amoros for the Great Catch in the 7th Game.

Brooklyn heroes: Roy Campanella and Johnny Podres

49

November 29, 1994

Dear Mr. Pesky:

I am a 34 year-old songwriter living in Los Angeles. I know your time is very valuable but I am curious as to who you would pick as your all time, all-star Red Sox team. Having really been such an integral part of the Sox for so many years, your picks would really be interesting.

My all time All Star Team.

INF.
1B – Jimmie Foxx
2B – Bobby Doerr
SS – Joe Cronin
3B – Frank Malzone
      Wade "Boggs"

C –
Carlton Fisk
Birdie Tebbetts

OF
Williams
Rice
Yastremski
Lynn
Evans

P.
RH Clemons – LH Parnell
RH Kinder – LH Hurst
RH.R Radatz –

Johnny Pesky

51

SAL DURANTE

Born 1941, Brooklyn, N.Y. He was the fan who on October 1, 1961 caught Roger Maris's 61st home run 15 rows up in the right-field stands at Yankee Stadium. That hit broke Babe Ruth's 1927 single-season record of 60 homers. At the time, Durante was 19, engaged to be married, and delivering auto parts. In exchange for the ball he received $5000 and two trips to the West Coast from a restaurateur. Today he resides in Brooklyn and drives a school bus.

Sal and his new pal

December 29, 1995

Dear Mr. Durante:

I recently read that you were the fan who caught Roger
Maris' 61st home run ball, on October 1, 1961, at
Yankee Stadium, to break Babe Ruth's single season
mark of 60. Wow!

Can you tell me if you were excited when Maris came to
bat,thinking he might hit the greatest home run ball
in the history of baseball to you? Can you still see
the ball coming at you when you think about that
moment? Finally,what did Maris say to you when you
gave him the ball after the game? I would be
fascinated to know your recollections sir.

Thank you very much for your time and have a very
happy New Year!

Sincerely,

Seth Swirsky

*Thinking back to the day I caught the ball,
the excitement was overwhelming.*

*I can still see the baseball in flight.
Hoping, I would be the one to catch it.*

*When I met Roger, the only thing I
wanted to do, was to give him the baseball.*

*He said, keep it and make some money.
I'll never forget what a great guy he was.*

*Sincerely
Sal Durant*

53

RALPH HOUK

Born 1919, Lawrence, Kansas. Catcher, 1947–1954; New York Yankees. Manager, 1961–1963, 1966–1978, 1981–1984; New York Yankees, Detroit Tigers, Boston Red Sox. In 1961, the year he took over as Yankee manager, Roger Maris and Mickey Mantle battled all summer for the home run crown, ultimately won by Maris with his record 61. I asked him if Mantle ever told him his feelings about Maris being the one to break the great record.

Dear Seth

In Regards To the question you Asked Me About Roger Maris" 61st Home Run:

Every one on the Team was pulling For Roger To get it, The quicker The better As we Were Looking For ward To the World Ser I Remember Mantle Telling me "I hope he gets it Today.

Of Course Every one in The dugout Was Excited And glad it was over so we Could Look For ward To The world series;

As Manager of the Team, I was happy because Now The press would let him Alone — he had been through a Lot the previous weeks,

My Best Regards.

Ralph Houk

Mgr. 61 N.y. yankees

54

Dear Leek

RECEIVED YOUR LETTER REQUESTING
info. on How my NAME ORIG-
iNATED. tHE oNLy thiNG i WAS
EVER toLD (By my MOTHER) tHAt OF
6 PREViOUS CHiLDReN my DAD WAS
NoT iNVOLVED iN NAMiNG ANy OF
tHEM. SO HE SUPPOSEDLy tRiED to
CAtCH UP, USiNG MEN HE NAMED
ME AFTER A PRESiDENt, A RoMAN,
EMPEROR AND AN iNDiAN CHiEF.
BEiNG PARt iNDiAN i GUESS HE
FELT HE HAD to GEt AN iNDiAN NAME
iN tHERE SOME WHERE- i'VE ALWAYS
CLAiMED HE HAD to BE iN tHE FiREWATER
to GiVE A KiD A NAME LiKE tHAt.
CALViN COOLiDGE WAS PRESiDENt WHEN
i WAS BORN (1925) DON't KNOW
WHERE JULiUS CAESAR CAME FRom.
tHAt'S ABOUt ALL i KNOW. i WAS
CALLED BUStER By ALL my FAMiLy.

REGARDS
Cal

CAL McLISH
Born 1925, Anadarko, Oklahoma. Righthanded pitcher, 1944, 1946–1949, 1951, 1956–1964; Cleveland Indians and
six other teams. He was the ace of the Cleveland pitching staff in 1958 and 1959, when he had a combined
record of 35 wins and 16 losses on his way to a 92-92 lifetime mark. I asked him the origin of his very
unusual name: Calvin Coolidge Julius Caesar Tuskahoma McLish.

January 21, 1995

Dear Mr. Auker:

Thank you very much for your letter about the '35
Tigers. It really gave me a new perspective on that
great team, one of real togetherness.

~~Again, I know your time is valuable but~~ I wanted to
follow-up by asking about the extent of the abuse Hank
Greenberg had to endure? From your perspective, did
players really get on him because he was Jewish and
who were they?

In the 6 years, Hank & I were playing for the Tigers, only one
incident occurred where his Jewish Heritage was ever noted.
This happened in about 1937 when we were playing the Chicago
White Sox in Detroit. Only Hank heard the remark after he
grounded out & was returning to our dugout. Evidently, someone
of the White Sox, called from the Bench, to Hanks back "you
Yellow Jew S-B-". Following the game, Hank walked into the
White Sox Clubhouse & said "the man that called me a "yellow
Jew S-B-", stand up — ~~nobody~~ stood up! That was the end.
The only time in 6 years, I ever saw or heard any slurring
remarks about Hank Greenberg. I hasten to add, the man
that made the remark was the smartest player on the White Sox
Club — Hank could & would have wiped up the Clubhouse floor with him

Elden Auker

56

Elden Auker

The great Hank Greenberg

August 5, 1995

Dear Mr. Rosen:

I am a 35 year-old songwriter living in Los Angeles. I
once read that Hank Greenberg was your idol growing up
and that he then became a good friend to you and
somewhat of a mentor. Being Jewish, I wondered if he
ever related any of his trials and tribulations of
being one of a handful of Jewish players in his time?
I truly would be fascinated to know if you decide to
jot down a note or two.

Again, Mr. Rosen, thank you very much for your time.
You were a great player!

Outside of our few years together, Hank
and I didn't see much of each other. As an aspiring
young player, I admired his exploits and chose him
as my "idol." We rarely discussed Anti-Semitism
as is applied to our careers. Undoubtedly it existed,
but our bent in life was to let our success disarm
any overt prejudice.
                                        with regards
                                        Al Rosen

NED GARVER
Born 1925, Ney, Ohio.
Righthanded pitcher,
1948–1961; St. Louis
Browns, Detroit Tigers
Kansas City Athletics, and
Los Angeles Angels. He
won 20 games for a
weak-hitting St. Louis
Browns team that lost 102
in 1951, on his way to a
career record of 129 wins
and 157 losses.

December 3, 1995

Dear Mr. Garver:

I love to study Baseball history and I just read about
that game you pitched on August 24, 1951 for the St.
Louis Browns against the Philadelphia team. That's the
game where your club-owner Bill Veeck gave 1115 fans
behind the dugout signs that read "Yes" and "No"
letting them decide the strategy in the game. How
funny! It says that the after you gave up 5 hits in
the first inning the "grandstand-managers" were asked
"Shall We Warm Up A New Pitcher?" and the fans
answered 'no'--you went on give up two more hits and won
5-3!

I wondered if you could tell me about that game and
Mr. Veeck--he sounds like he was really having fun
as an owner.

[handwritten note]

Seth—
Bill Veeck was in a class by himself. Had more
promotional ideas every day than most owners had
in their lifetime. He loved Baseball + would do nothing to
hurt it. Not the case today. Sad — sad — sad. He might
trade you tomorrow but when you played for him, he made
you feel 10' tall.

The thing I remember about Grandstand
managers nite was in the sat inning—runs in—
still men on 1st + 2nd — only one out—they voted to
bring the infield in; Sherm Lollar — my catcher — came out to see
and stalled until Zack Taylor finally got an infield back "vote.
I then got a ground ball for a double play to end the inning."

Ned

59

October 6, 1995

Dear Mr. Pearson:

I wondered if you could tell me if you ever met President Eisenhower when you played for the Washington Senators in the late 50's? Was it exciting to play in front of the President?

DEAR SETH—

I DIDN'T HAVE THE PLEASURE OF MEETING "IKE" until 1/1962 WHEN I WAS WITH THE ANGELS. WE WERE TRAINING IN PALM SPRINGS NEAR HIS HOME, THE EL DORADO CC IN INDIAN WELLS. HE BECAME A "REAL" ANGEL FAN, ATTENDING MANY "SPRING" GAMES.

IN 1963 I HAD THE PLEASURE OF PLAYING A LITTLE GOLF AND PRESENTING HIM A SILVER BAT AS THE ANGELS "#1 FAN". HE WAS A VERY GRACIOUS AND SPECIAL PERSON.

PERSONAL REGARDS TO YOU SETH AND GOD BLESS YOU
ISIAH 9:6 Albie Pearson

62

September 25, 1995

Dear Mr. Stevens:

I wondered if you could tell me what it was like to play
baseball in your day?

Thank you for your time and have a nice day!

Very Sincerely,

Seth Swirsky

In my day (1925-1934) baseball underwent big change. Night baseball crept in slowly. The lights were terrible in the beginning. Nothing, really, can take the place of the sun. Gloves were smaller in my day. Travel was by train in the AA leagues and the big leagues. At Newark in the Int League (AA) we had two Pullmans; at Phila (Nat League) we had one Pullman.

Good luck —

Bob Stevens

Phils 1931

DICK WILLIAMS
Born 1928, St. Louis, Missouri. Utility player, 1951–1964; Brooklyn Dodgers, Baltimore Orioles, and three other teams. Manager, 1967–1969, 1971–1988. Although he played for 13 years, he made his mark as a highly successful manager, winning 1571 games in 21 years. Despite frequent run-ins with his players, he piloted four teams to the World Series: the '67 Red Sox, the '72 and '73 Oakland A's, and the '84 San Diego Padres.

January 5, 1995

Dear Mr. Williams:

I have always loved the '67 Red Sox and in retrospect it really is quite amazing what you did with that team, coming just a victory away from a championship in your first season at the helm.

I wonder if you could tell me what was it about that team that made it so special? Also, did Conigliaro's injury hurt the team down the stretch?

The 1967 Red Sox were a young group of players who never experienced winning before and what it took to reach that goal — I was very hard and demanding on the players and at times we had very strained relations but they found out it took hard work plus the talent to be successful. Replacing Conigliaro was very hard and seven (7) different players played there after he went down. His talent was special!

D.W.

ny C. after the Beantown beaning

February 14, 1995

Dear Mr. Lonborg:

I really started to follow baseball as a seven year-old in 1967, the year the Red Sox had that special team. I wondered if you could tell me if you were nervous when you took the mound for the seventh game of the '67 Series? Did you and Yaz talk strategy before the game? I truly would appreciate your recollection.

Dear Seth,

I wasn't actually nervous before the seventh game. I had faced the Cardinals twice in games 2 & 5 and beat them. I was actually more fatigued than nervous and was hoping we'd score some early runs off Bob Gibson.

I spent more time with my catcher before the game to develop strategy. We knew how to get the hitters out. We just didn't know how my arm would feel after only two days rest. Jim Lonborg

July 8, 1995

Dear Mr. Briles:

I always liked you as a player, but I have to admit, when I saw on the back of your baseball card back in 1969, that your birthday was the same as mine (August 5th), you were instantly one of my favorites! I have always thought that the '67 and'68 St. Louis Cardinals were one of the great teams in the history of baseball. I wondered if you could tell me did Northrup's triple in game 7 come as a shock to you and your teammates?

Seth—

Happy Birthday! I am Director of Corporate Relations with the Pirates so I'm still involved with major league baseball. As to your question about Northrup's line drive triple in game seven of the '68 World Series — I thought Curt Flood was going to catch the ball until he slipped trying to go back A the ball. My heart sank as I then realized we were not going to repeat as world champions!

Life goes on!! Have a glass of wine for me!

Nellie Briles

TOT PRESNELL
Born 1906, Findlay, Ohio.
Righthanded pitcher, 1938–
1942; Brooklyn Dodgers and
Chicago Cubs. He was a
knuckleballer whose locker
was right next to Babe Ruth's
when a retired Babe was
third-base coach for the
Dodgers in 1938.

October 11, 1995

Dear Mr. Presnell:

I am a 35 year-old songwriter living in Los Angeles. I love to read about the history of baseball and I wondered if you could tell me (below) what kind of guy the great Babe Ruth was--didn't you play on the Dodgers when Ruth was a coach for them in 1938? Did he really want to be a manager as bad as everyone says he did?

I don't believe Babe ever wanted to be a manger. He would never be a manager, 'cause he could not remember signs. He never had one sign to remeber. Couldn't remember names. Everyone knows Babe was a hard drinker, You might call him a lone wolf. Away from the park, We never saw him.

PAUL HOPKINS
Born 1904, Chester, Pennsylvania. Pitcher, 1927, 1929; Washington Senators, St. Louis Browns. On September 29, 1927, rookie Paul Hopkins, pitching for the Senators, gave up home run #59 to Babe Ruth in the Babe's record-setting 60-home-run year. I wondered what he remembered about facing Ruth.

Paul Hopkins

HOPKINS

over

6/12/95

Dear Seth,

Re — 59ᵗʰ H.R.
To Babe Ruth (1927)
my 1st appearance
in majors with
2 out, bases loaded
2 + 3 on hitter +
then the baseball
lands in 4 or 5ᵗʰ
row. after inn-
ing only on way
to bench my
eyes were a bit wet

e Babe

Dear Mr. Hauser: January 21, 1995

You really had a very interesting career. I wonder if you could
tell me two things:

1) Do you think you could have broken Ruth's record of 60
   home runs in a season?

2) Why were the Minors more fun than the Majors for you?

Dear Seth:

*#1, I broke
the Babs record of 61 home
runs 2 times allready,
I got 63 homers at Baltimore
International League, and
69 homers at Minneapolis
in 1933- American Association
both teams were playing Triple
A- Baseball next to the Big Leagues,
surprising you to ask me to
to break Ruths record of 61 homers
I done broke his record 2 times
once in 1930 & the other time in
1933 at Minneapolis, 1930 at
Baltimore, surprising you ask
a question of that was broken
over 50 yrs. ago Baseball is all-
ways fun minor or Major League
hope you are satisfied for my
answer.*

*Kindest Regards-
Joe Hauser*

74

JOE HAUSER
Born 1899, Milwaukee, Wisconsin.
First baseman, 1922–1924, 1926,
1928–1929; Philadelphia Athletics,
Cleveland Indians. He was brought
up to the majors in 1922 with much
fanfare as a home run hitter who
could challenge Babe Ruth. He came
in second in the home run race in
1924, hitting 27 to Ruth's 46. In
1930 a knee injury forced him to
the minor leagues, where he hit
more than 60 home runs in two
different seasons—the only man
ever to hit over sixty home runs
twice in organized ball.

Dear Baseball Fan,

I regret to inform you that Jack Wilson passed away on April 19, 1995.

He was always honored to receive requests for his autograph on anything that was sent to him. It was a great source of pride for him to have anyone ask for his signature. Jack loved baseball and the baseball fan and I am sure he would wish you best of times and enjoy baseball.

My best to you and your family,

Sincerely yours,

Mrs Jack Wilson

Mrs. Jack Wilson

June 25, 1995

Dear Mr. Staley:

I have a baseball signed by Ernie Banks and I wondered if you would sign it too?   Of course, I would pay you whatever fee you asked and include a return mailer. I truly would appreciate it sir.

✓ I can sign the ball. ~~My fee is $~~_____ *I don't charge for autographs. I feel honored to be asked. I'm just thankful to be alive and able to do it*

___ I cannot sign the ball now

Jerry Staley

JIM KAAT
Born 1938, Zeeland, Michigan.
Lefthanded pitcher,
1959– 1983; Minnesota Twins.
The winningest pitcher in
Twins history, he pitched
during a record-tying seven
presidential administrations.
He won 283 games and his
16 straight Gold Glove awards
makes it clear why he is
often regarded as the greatest
fielding pitcher ever.

May 26, 1995

Dear Mr. Kaat:

I wondered if you could tell me what was the greatest
game that your father saw you pitch and were you
nervous?

JIM KAAT

6/29/95

Seth,

He saw me pitch Game
2 of the 1965 World Series.
We beat Sandy Koufax
and the Dodgers that day
5-1.

I was not any more
nervous than any other game
It was a great Father-Son
"feeling" because he was such
a baseball fan.

Sincerely,
Jim Kaat

WHITEY FORD
Born 1926, New York, New York. Lefthanded pitcher, 1950, 1953–1967; New York Yankees. Hall of Fame, 1974. When the "Chairman of the Board" took the mound, the Yankees usually won. He holds almost all the major World Series records for pitchers—wins, strikeouts, innings pitched, etc. I wondered if, like other boys of his era growing up in New York, he made Joe DiMaggio his hero, and whether he ever saw him play.

Joe

Dec 5, 1996

Dear Seth

When I was 10 yrs. old, I went to see Joe DiMaggio at Yankee Stadium for the first time. Little did I think that eleven yrs. later he would be playing centerfield for me in my first start as a Yankee in 1950.

I was so in awe of him, that it was many years later before I felt comfortable having a chat with him.

He was one of the greatest!

All the best

Whitey Ford

AL MILNAR

Born 1913, Cleveland, Ohio. Lefthanded pitcher, 1936, 1938–1943, 1946; Cleveland Indians and two other teams. "Happy" was the pitcher who gave up the last hit of Joe DiMaggio's storied 56-game hitting streak in 1941. He also surrendered hits in games #17 and #29 of the streak. I asked him for his recollections of the Yankee Clipper's historic feat.

JOE DIMAGGIO

Pitching to one of the great hitters in baseball in a way makes me proud of my luck againest Joe Dimaggio in his amazing streak of 56 games in a row I can't say in truth I remember the hits Joe got in the streak in 1941- June 16 he had 1 for 4 June 23 he hit 1-for 5 a double July 16 he hit 2 for 3. His No 56 was a ground ball hit in front of the batters box hit hard with over spin to my right and Boudreau's left he came close to catching it. He had to play Joe to pull me and we missed by a step or two. Joe had 4 hits for 11 off me. He hit 408 in his streak He was stopped by Al Smith and Jim Bagby Jr. There were two great plays by Ken Kelkner and Lou Boudreau to end it. Joe had 15 more games in a row after No 56. I can't see how it will ever be broken

Dear Seth:

As you can see by my autograph
I no longer handle a pen well. So my
wife is my "write arm". My thôts, her pen.

Playing for the Yankees is a feeling
that can't be told. Only those of us who
have been fortunate enough to do it can
know the wonder of it. I know the game
& the players have changed – remember I
was there almost 50 years ago. And my
locker was next to Joe the Maggio. I was
given my idols #3 to wear – Talk about
"in awe of"! I'm not saying all the
guys were "saints" but there was a
team spirit, family atmosphere,
All professionals. The Magg could ~~say~~
get his point across just with a look. He

played his heart out & expected the same of everyone else. Charlie Keller was a wonderful example of what a man could & should be. Our pitchers, the late Raschi (my roomie) Reynolds (my good friend) & Lopat were wonderful - All were 'Stars' but they were part of the team just like everyone else - As for a man in a clutch - Tom Henrich was it - If you needed a hit ~~a hit~~

you called on Tommy - Seems like no matter who was ~~needed~~ called on - they could do the job -

Those were wonderful years & I'm so grateful I shared them - The memories keep me going —

As for your being a songwriter - I can't imagine how you do what you do. I love music - Not all of it - but my cupboard is full of 40's-50's & a little 60's type. My wife likes the words - I'll take the instrumentals - Hope your career as a songwriter will be fulfilling to you —

Sincerely —

Cliff

85

August 12, 1995

Dear Mr. Raffensberger:

I looked up your Major League Career record and it says
that you were the MVP of the '44 All-Star game. I wondered
if you could tell me (below) if your parents and other
family were at that game to watch your great performance?
What did you do after the game?

Hi Seth :,

You better bet my parents were at the
game, along with my 4 brothers, as
Pittsburgh is only 200 mile from
York.

I probably went along home with my
parents, as we didn't play till Thurs.
And Phila. is only 90 mile from York.

Kindest Regards

Ken Raffensberger

August 17, 1995

Dear Mr. Underwood:

I read recently that you pitched against your brother in
his pitching debut in the Majors-- May 31, 1979. You both
pitched brilliantly in the game.

I wondered if you could tell me if you gave him any advice
before the game and if you spoke after the contest?

I TOLD HIM WE WOULD BE ON CENTER STAGE
TONIGHT, THROUGHOUT THE COUNTRY, NOT JUST IN TORONTO.
SO LET'S GIVE THEM A SHOW. AFTERWARDS, I TOLD HIM
I WAS VERY PROUD OF HIM. HE'S WAS & STILL IS MY
BEST FRIEND.

Tom Underwood

TOM UNDERWOOD
Born 1953, Kokomo,
Indiana. Lefthanded
pitcher, 1974–1984;
Oakland A's and five
other teams. He faced
his younger brother
Pat in the latter's
pitching debut, losing
a hard-fought 1-0
game.

AL KALINE
Born 1934, Baltimore, Maryland. Outfielder, 1953–1974; Detroit Tigers. Hall of Fame, 1980. One of the all-time great Tigers, at 20 he became the youngest batting champion ever, hitting .340. He hit over .300 nine times, had 3007 hits and 399 home runs, and won 10 Gold Gloves. In his only World Series, in 1968, he hit .379 with two home runs to lead the Tigers to their dramatic comeback victory.

February 11, 1995

Dear Mr. Kaline:

I wondered if you could tell me what was the highest high
you had in your amazing career and what was the greatest
single disappointment?

High - Was to play on the world champion Detroit Tigers in '68
Also just to play in the Big Leagues for 22 years

Lowest disappointment - a lost on the last day of the
season in 1967 and lose to Boston for the AL Championship.

Al Kaline

GEORGE KELL
Born 1922, Swifton, Arkansas. Third baseman, 1943–
1957; Detroit Tigers, Baltimore Orioles, and three other
teams. Hall of Fame, 1983. A great defensive player, he
hit over .300 for eight consecutive years ('46–'53),
leading the league in 1949 with .343. Traded to the
Baltimore Orioles in 1956, he took a young fellow
Arkansan named Brooks Robinson under his wing. I
wondered what the great veteran third baseman
thought when he saw the third baseman of the
future.

DETROIT BASEBALL COMPANY 3-1-95
DETROIT, MICHIGAN

Dear Seth –
I first saw Brooks Robinson when
I was traded to Baltimore – that was mid
year 1956 – He came to spring training in
1957 – And I had been told he could handle
the glove as well as any one – and boy
could he ever – I don't think he ever got
a whole lot better with the glove – because
he was picture perfect then.

90

He opened the season with us and played good – when a left hander pitched Brooks played third & I moved to first base – but he was young – swung at a lot of bad pitches – so about the All Star Game Paul Richards sent him back to play every day – when he came back to stay two years later – he was a polished Major League Ball play – And of course went on to become a good clutch hitter – I did nothing to help him play – He was quoted once as saying I taught him how to act like a Major Leaguer – I liked that very much – We remain Great friends today –

Sincerely

George Kell

BROOKS ROBINSON
Born 1937, Little Rock, Arkansas.
Third baseman, 1955–1977;
Baltimore Orioles. Hall of Fame,
1983. The greatest-fielding third
baseman in the history of the
game, the "human vacuum cleaner"
earned 16 Gold Gloves for his
defensive prowess. For his entire
23-year career he played for the
Baltimore Orioles, belting 268 home
runs and a total of 2848 hits in
10,654 at-bats. He was the 1964
American League MVP and the
1970 World Series MVP. I asked
him what influence George Kell
had had on him.

Dear Seth, Sorry this letter is so tardy. I kept getting away with a few other things.

George Kell was one of two idols I had as a youngster growing up in Arkansas. I use to follow all of the big league players from Arkansas, knowing their stats and where they came from etc.

My rookie year 1957 was George Kells last year. In fact, opening game in Washington D.C.'s Griffin Stadium, I played 3rd for the Orioles and George played first. George was a big influence in my life. George and his wife just kind of took me under their wing and showed me what being a big leaguer was all about. In fact, he took me to my first stage play in New York.

There has never been a more finer gentleman to put on a big league uniform than George. It was my good fortune to have him there in 1957 on the field and off. I tried to emulate him in many ways.

And then the most exciting part was going into the Hall of Fame together in 1983. Could it get any hotter? A perfect ending.

Thanks,
Brooks

MARTY MARION
Born 1917, Richburg, South Carolina. Shortstop, 1940–1950, 1952–1953; St. Louis Cardinals, St. Louis Browns. "Slats," the first shortstop to be chosen the National League's Most Valuable Player, in 1944, helped lead his Cardinals to three World Championships—in 1942, 1944, and 1946. As his teammate Enos Slaughter raced home with the winning run of the 1946 World Series, Marion was on deck, getting a great look at the decisive play.

June 15, 1995

Dear Mr. Marion:

Enclosed is that fabulous picture of Enos Slaughter sliding in with the run that gave the '46 Cardinals the series. I wonder if you would sign it Marty 'Slats' Marion (isn't that what they called you sir?).

Also, looking at the picture, can you tell me what you were thinking and feeling at the time. I truly would love to know.

Dear Seth –
To tell the truth – I don't know what I was thinking – ?

Marty

94

os Slaughter completes his "Mad Dash" as Marion looks on.

BUDDY HASSETT
Born 1911, New York City. First baseman, 1936–1942; Brooklyn Dodgers, Boston Braves, and New York Yankees. A consistent performer, Hassett hit below .284 in only one of his seven seasons, maintaining a career average of .292 in 3,517 at-bats.

March 7, 1995

Dear Mr. Hassett:

I am a 34 year-old songwriter living in Los Angeles. I know your time is very valuable but I wondered if you could tell me (below), what the difference between playing for the Dodgers, Braves and Yankees were? Who had the best fans and which team had the most 'fun' together? I truly would appreciate your response sir.

I've enclosed self-addressed, stamped envelope for your convenience if you decide to jot down a note or two.

Very Sincerely,

Seth Swirsky
Seth Swirsky

Playing for the Yankees was by far the most fun because you were winning most of the time.
Brooklyn had the best fans by far.
Boston had the most polite and 2nd best fans

Buddy Hassett

97

August 21, 1995

Der Mr. Landrith:

I recently read you were there when the Reds had a promo-
tion to drop a baseball 575 from a helicopter and have their
catchers catch it! When you saw the first one fall and go six
inches into the ground, did you decide not to do it? Did you
actually try to catch one?

Seth —

The Reds were playing the Giants that night and Leo Durocher would <u>not</u> let his catchers try to catch the ball after seeing the 1st ball dropped bury in the outfield grass. Yes, I ~~try~~ tried it. I had a bet of free cokes with my team mates that I would touch one of the three attempts. I won the bet, but did n't catch one. The helicopter was lowered to 550 feet and I caught the last ball dropped. It felt like a sledge hammer hitting my mitt. It was fun. It was a real spectacle.

all the best!
Hobie Landrith

JOE GINSBERG
Born 1926, New York
City. Catcher, 1948,
1950–1954, 1956–1962;
Baltimore Orioles and
six other teams. He
was the Mets' opening-
day catcher in 1962.

August 24, 1995

Dear Mr. Ginsberg:

I enjoy reading about baseball history and came across the funny
story of how Paul Richards, your manager with the '57 Orioles,
suggested that because a catchers mitt was not well-suited to
make a "play at the plate" you, the team's catcher, switch gloves
with the pitcher while the runner is rounding the bases headed
for home on a hit to the outfield. I know you practiced this play
and tried it, but the pitcher that day was Bill Wight, a lefty,
and you were before 30,000 trying to make a play with the wrong-
handed mitt!! I know your time is very valuable, but I wondered
if you could tell me what you said to Manager Richards when you
came to the dugout and did your teammates ever rib you about it?

THE STORY IS TRUE, I USE IT AT
OUTING's & DINNER'S, YES, I TOOK A
LOT OF HEAT FROM MY TEAM MATES, BUT
BEING A CATCHER, THEY KNOW THE
PERIL'S OF THE JOB, SO THEY STOP very
FAST.

FRED LYNN
Born 1952, Chicago, Illinois. Outfielder,
1974–1990; Boston Red Sox, California Angels,
and three other teams. In 1975, he became the
only rookie ever to win the Most Valuable
Player award, hitting .331 with 21 home runs
and 103 runs batted in. An excellent defensive
center fielder, his impressive career totals
include 306 home runs and a .283 average.

January 4, 1995

Dear Mr. Lynn:

Although I grew up in New York, I always admired the '75 Red Sox. I
wondered who was your idol growing up and did you ever get to meet
him and talk about baseball?

Dear Seth,
    My favorite player was Willie
Mays. I met him once, but we
talked about golf & not baseball.
    Best of luck with your songwriting.
        Fred Lynn

2-1-95

Dear Seth,

Since I pitched the last game of the '69 series, I was on the mound when Cleon caught the ball for the final out, & J. Grote was the 1st person I jumped on & hugged.

Sincerely

Jerry Koosman

P.S. Thanks for your nice letter.

1/21/95

Dear Seth,
    1969 was a wonderful season! Most of us seemed to move through that season as if we were dreaming. Why! Gil Hodges.
    He was our inspiration and guide. He knew what he was doing and we followed. The games are well documented.
    All of us call recall incidents that we individually felt cause our success.
    1969 was the legacy Gil Hodges left all of us.
                    # 3
                    Buddy Harrelson

BUD HARRELSON
Born 1944, Niles, California. Shortstop, 1965–1980; New York Mets and two other teams. The Mets shortstop in 1969 and 1973, and their third-base coach in 1986, Harrelson was the only Met to be in uniform for all 19 games of their three World Series. I asked him if there was one '69 Met who was indispensable to that team's success.

ART SMITH
Born 1906, Boston,
Massachusetts. Right-
handed pitcher, 1932;
Chicago White Sox. His
entire career consisted
of three games, includ-
ing two starts. He had
one decision—a loss—
and one strikeout.

September 25, 1995

Dear Mr. Smith:

I wondered if you could tell me (below) what it was like to play baseball in your day?

From 1928 to 1933 I played professional ball, mostly minor league, with a brief stay with the White Sox in 1932. This was before the time of Jackie Robinson. From 1934 to 1941 I played with an all-white semi-pro team in the New York City area. We played 50% of our games with the teams in the negro National League. They had players that should have been in the big leagues. Josh Gibson, Satchel Paige, Cool Papa Bell, Cannon ball Redding, Charleston, Thomas, Leonard (can't remember the first names). I'm so glad they broke the color line years ago — because playing in the big leagues should be based on ability — not race. Did you see the Yankee–Seattle series? Broke my heart — but the better team won.
Yours in baseball — Art Smith

VIRGIL TRUCKS
Born 1919, Birmingham, Alabama. Righthanded pitcher, 1941–1943, 1945–1958; Detroit Tigers and four other teams. "Fire" compiled a solid 177-135 record with a 3.39 E.R.A., but his worst season, 1952, was his most interesting: Pitching on the worst team in Detroit Tiger history, he won 5 and lost 19. Remarkably, two of those five victories were no-hitters, one was a one-hitter, and another was a two-hitter! I asked him to tell me about the first game he ever pitched in the big leagues.

FROM THE MOUND OF

VIRGIL 'FIRE' TRUCKS

My first major league game I pitched in Fenway Park in Boston. Johnny Pesky was the lead off hitter. On my first pitch he singled. Bobby Doerr, the 2nd hitter hit my 1st pitch for a double. Ted Williams the 3rd hitter hit the first pitch I threw to him for a double. Steve O'Neal the manager for us called time, meeting with and the catcher Bob Swift at the mound. Steve never spoke to me, he said to Bob Swift the catcher, Say Bob, doesn't Virgil have it to-day. And Bob answered, How the hell do I know. I haven't caught a pitch yet. a true story. by. Virgil Trucks

PITCHED NO-HITTER VS. WASHINGTON SENATORS 1-0, MAY 15. 1952
PITCHED NO-HITTER VS. NEW YORK YANKEES 1-0, AUGUST 25. 1952

JIMMY WYNN
Born 1942, Hamilton, Ohio. Outfielder, 1963–1977; Houston Astros, L.A. Dodgers, and three other teams. At five-feet-ten and 160 pounds, the "Toy Cannon" belted 291 career home runs, with seven seasons of more than 20 homers. I asked him about the greatest moments in his career.

Dear Seth
    My Greatest Moment in sports were my two years at Central State College, in Wilberforce, Ohio, and my signing of my professional Baseball contract with the Cincinnati Reds, and to see the tears come down my father's cheeks, that was the crowning moments of hard work and dedication, for a future of baseball my <u>Desire</u>

Jim Wynn
"Toy Cannon"

109

January 9, 1995

Dear Mr. Jenkins:

Growing up, I was a big Met fan and remember well the exciting pennant race in 1969 with the Cubs. You were a tremendous competitor sir, but I think that all of the personal hardship you have had to overcome in recent years shows what a truly amazing person you are! Your induction to the Hall of Fame in '91 was overdue and well-deserved.

I wondered if you could tell me what was your highest high as a player and your lowest low.

1 - my highest high was having 6 strikeouts in an all-star game in Anaheim 1967.

2 - '91 Induction into the "Hall of Fame."

3 - Winning 20 games 6 yrs. in a row for the Chicago Cubs.

4 - Lowest part of my career was the trade from the Philly's in 1966. I was 21 yr. old.

111

May 4, 1995

Dear Mr. Osteen:

I always thought that your record of 196-195 could very easily have been 300-100 if you had been on slightly better hitting teams. I know your time is very valuable, but I wondered if you could tell me (below) what was your happiest moment in baseball? Were you ever standing on the mound, on a beautiful day, and just say to yourself--this is amazing!?

I think my happiest moment in baseball was putting a Cincinnati Reds uniform on directly at the age of 17 out of high school and going straight to the M.L.

I've had many great moments; my first time wearing the Dodger uniform, 1st World Series start, win & shutout. Its very difficult to single one out.

Many times I've had the thoughts " a beautiful day, this is amazing" while standing on the mound at Dodger stadium.

Claude Osteen

112

July 5, 1995

Dear Mr. Sherry:

I recently read an account of how Sandy Koufax went
from a wild, overthrowing fastballer to one of the games
great hurlers after you had a talk with him in 1961.

I wonder if you could tell me (below) what you saw that
others hadn't? Also, did you look forward to catching
Sandy as opposed to some of the other pitchers?

IN ANSWER To your ABOVE QuesTion About what I
knew that others Hadn't, WAS Nothing MECHANICAL, I JUST Sugested to
him NoT To Try To THrow his FAST AS Hand AS He Could. INSTead
Try To throw A 100 MPH do it At 95. So Much His ConTrol
better.
Sandy WAS easy to caTch As other PiTchers,
did NoT Have The SreaT ConTrol He came to Have - Also His
F.B. WAS light with A liTTle Rise to it. Some piTchers HAve
Heavy F.B And sinking action.

113

January 14, 1995

Dear Mr. Rigney:

I remember you as a manager, as I started really getting into baseball at age 9, in 1969. But, I wanted to ask you a question about
when you were a player, a N.Y. Giant: where were you and what were
you thinking when Bobby Thomson hit his famous home run to take the
pennant in '51? Who was the first person you hugged on the field?

Seth — I was in the clubhouse —
1st person I hugged was Horace
Stoneham, the owner —
I had helped carry Don Mueller off
the field in the 9th —
Ben Bill Rigney

February 6, 1995

Dear Mr. Mueller:

In the 3rd game of the '51 playoffs, after Rigney had taken you off the field, how did you find out about Thomson's home run—did you hear the fans cheer? Where were you and were you in a lot of pain? I would be fascinated to know how word of his home run and the Giants big victory came to you.

Friend Seth,

When I broke my ankle I was carried to the clubhouse, which was in center field. Lying on the training table, no radio. no one to talk to. I heard a roar. it could mean 1 of 2 things. win or lose. and then the players came & were loud and laughing. Then I knew. my ankle had swollen the size of a Football. But victory erased the pain.

my best to you
friend
Don Mueller

February 21, 1995

Dear Mr. Irvin:

I wondered if you could tell me what your highest high was as a player and also, what was your greatest disappointment?

My greatest thrill was stealing home in the first inning of the 1951 World Series game against the Yankees.

My biggest disappointment was not winning the M.V.P. of the National League in 1951.

Monte Irvin

January 24, 1995

Dear Mr. Spahn:

Did you know how great Willie Mays would be when he got his first
career home run off of you? Looking back, it truly was a
historic at-bat--two future Hall-of-Famers. I wondered if you
could tell me what you remember about that at-bat.

I remember very well May- first
at bat. The information we had was that
he pulled away from the plate when he
swung & that he couldn't reach the curve
ball on the outside. The pitch he hit
off me was a curve ball on the outside
curver but from a left hander, he didn't
Pull away & thus the homerun

Warren Spahn

MICKEY HAEFNER
Born 1912, Lenzburg, Illinois.
Died 1995. Lefthanded pitcher,
1943–1950; Washington Senators and two other teams. A
starting pitcher, he had his
best year as a rookie in 1943,
when he won 11 games and
lost 5 with a 2.29 E.R.A.

May 22, 1995

Dear Mr. Haefner:

I have a baseball that I want to get signed by all
the "Mickeys"-- Yourself,Mantle,Owen,Lolich, etc.

Obviously, I would love if you could sign my "Mickey"
ball. I would be honored to have you on the ball sir.

Of course, any fee that you might want to sign, I will
oblige. And I will send a return pre-paid mailer.

Thank you again for your time sir and I really hope
that you have time sign my ball.

Very Sincerely,

Seth Swirsky

Dear Seth:-
Mickey passed away Jan 3/95. He suffered a
stroke in Jan of 1989 and it left him totally helpless.
He was in nursing home here in New Athens so I
could be with him each day. I miss him very much but
thank the Lord for taking him home - 6 yrs was enough.
He was a gentle man - good husband (58 yrs) and
wonderful father.   Thank You
for your interest in him - makes me happy to know so
many remember him. He loved the game of baseball. Lucille (wife)

August 3, 1995

Dear Mr. Ashburn:

I just wanted to tell you that I saw your induction to the Hall
of Fame this past week and was moved to tears by your beautiful
acceptance speech. What a thrill it must have been to have your
91 year-old mother there!

I wondered if you could tell me did your mother encourage you to
play ball as a youth and did you ever call her during your
career to tell her of your accomplishments?

My mother and
father were great
"Cheerleaders" during my
youth — not only for me
but also my brother and
sisters

My mother followed
my career very closely —
travelled and has
always been close to
my career
accomplishments

R.A.

December 27, 1994

Dear Mr. Feller:

Who was your idol as a boy and did you ever pitch to him?

Dear Seth:

Rogers Hornsby was my idol. I wanted to play 2nd base + did in American Legion Baseball before at age 15 pitched most of the time.

I pitched To Rogers Hornsby while he managed the St. Browns in 1936.

Sincerely Yours,

Bob Feller

January 3, 1995

Dear Mr. Nonnenkamp:

I am a 34 year-old songwriter living in Los Angeles. I
know your time must be valuable but I wondered if you
could tell me what it was like playing baseball when
you played? Who were some of the best you saw in those
years? I truly would appreciate your response.

Dear Seth:—   1/16/95
          So many changes in the game today.
Equiptment, — play ing fields, are so much better.
Can't brag on the hours they play. Prefer our
schedule — afternoon games, Then an enjoyable
dinner. More relaxing and less tension. Some better now,
financially. Would n't be surprised, to read how that
money is spent. Not much salary bargaining back then.
Not so many teams in the Major Leagues, and so many
more teams in the Minor league. So it was take what
was offered, Or.

          Red Sox had quite a few established stars in '38.
All were pretty friendly, but the extra players usually
went our own way. Lefty Grove was at the end of his

124

LEO NONNENKAMP
Born 1911, St. Louis, Missouri. Outfielder, 1933, 1938–1940; Boston Red Sox and one other team. "Red" was a lefty-swinging outfielder who played alongside some of the all-time greats—Jimmie Foxx, Lefty Grove, Ted Williams, and Bobby Doerr. In 1938, his best year, he hit .283.

career - still he was real crafty. Foxx, Vosmik, Ben Chapman, Cramer - Higgens, Cronin all established stars, so they were never the rah-rah type. Maybe that is why Boston usually finished second to the Yankees. Bobby Doerr and Ted Williams were just breaking in - but didn't they both have outstanding careers?? Williams got all the attention, from all the players, when hitting, whether in a game or just batting practice. I would pick him as the best hitter, ever.!!! Quite a thrill to visit all the parks. Yankee Stadium was super. Made you feel so small. Boston drew well there - quite a bit of rivalry between the teams. And so many of the better players, on both teams, Lou Gehrig, Ruth, Muesel, Ruffing, Gomez, Gordon, Rolfe and the best catcher in baseball - Bill Dickey.

    Enjoyed my short stay, especially, when Ben Chapman came up sickly - that meant, I would have a chance to play. Would have been more to my liking, if I could have taken advantage of the opportunity.

    Watch some T.V. games. We have a team here in LR, in the Texas League, sponsored by the St. L. Cardinals. Stay for about five innings - nite games get pretty late for this old-goat,

                Sincerely
                  Leo

May 26, 1995

Dear Mr. Thomas:

I am a 34 year-old songwriter living in Los Angeles. I
know your time is very valuable, but I wondered if you
could tell me (below) if you remember the great Ted
Williams at-bat against you on April 23, 1939 when he
hit his very first of 512 career home runs? What was
that at-bat like from your perspective?
be fascinated to know sir.

Ted Williams Hit His first
Home Run off Me in april
1939, in Boston. made me feel Bad
at the time, But after the years
went own, I dident feel So Bad.

Good Luck
"Bud" Thomas

126

February 16, 1995

Dear Mr. Shantz:

I wondered if you could tell me what you felt when you found out you had been traded to the Yankees?

BOBBY SHANTZ
Born 1925, Pottstown, Pennsylvania. Lefthanded pitcher, 1949–1964; Philadelphia Athletics, N.Y. Yankees, and six other teams. A superb fielding pitcher, he was the American League MVP in 1952, posting a 24-7 record with the A's. Traded to the Yankees in 1957, he led the league with a 2.45 E.R.A. He was an asset on every team he pitched for; I asked him if it was different to pitch for the Yankees.

Dear Seth,

Like I said, playing for the Yankees was the best 4 years of my baseball life. When pitching against the Yankees, I always thought I really done something special when I beat the powerful Yankees. In 1952 I beat them 4 times and one of those games was a 14 inning complete game in Yankee stadium. When it was all over that day, I really couldn't believe I pitched the whole game and beat them.

When I was traded to them in 1957, I felt like running all the way up to New York. Pitching for them was really great because I always knew I was going to get some runs and their defense was very good also. There was always a very good chance to get in the World Series also, which we did 3 of the 4 years I spent with them. A wonderful experience!! Also had the roommate of the century in Bobby Richardson. What a great guy!

Sincerely,
Bobby Shantz

127

Bobby Richardson

Just a note Jett

To say thanks for your letter & especially the words about Mantle's funeral.

My Dad did get To see me play on Television for several years Via SAT. games & World Series. I wish his health had allowed more than the 1 game that I played 3rd Base.

Over the years the liner by Mc Covey seems To pick up Speed & a much more difficult play. That's True when y are looking Back.

— Thanks again —

Bob Richardson —

December 26, 1995

Dear Mr. Rogell:

I wondered if you could tell me about a play that happened in the '34 World Series when you played shortstop for the great Tigers against the "Gas House Gang" Cardinals in 1934.

Dizzy Dean, on sliding into 2nd base in game five, was hit in the head with the baseball and carried off the field. Do you remember the play and did you overhear any conversation while they were tending to Dizzy?

ell checks dizzy Dizzy

Dizzy Dean - did not slide
He came standing up. and
after he came too Fust thing
he said. How did I brake up
the double play? He was lucky
that I did not throw the ball
as hard as I could - Frisch should
of had his head examined why he
let Dizzy run

The Dodger "Infield of Dreams"—Ron Cey, Bill Russell, Davey Lopes, Steve Garvey

January 24, 1995

Dear Mr. Cey:

I am a thirty-four year-old songwriter living in Los
Angeles. I know your time is very valuable, but I
wondered if you could tell me (below) if you felt
'Dodger tradition' while you were playing for them?
Was it the same to play for Chicago or Oakland or was
there something tangibly different playing for the
Dodgers? I truly would appreciate your reply.

Hi Seth,

There was always a sense of responsibility to live up to the Dodger tradition. To try and stay on a level of past Dodger teams and players that became World Champions and Hall of Famers was an honor not a burden.

I believe we held our own by playing in four World Series and winning a World Championship in my ten years in Los Angeles.

Best Regards!

Ron Cey

December 21, 1994

Dear Mr. Garvey:

While Reggie Jackson gets all the accolades for performing so well in World Series play, I don't think anyone touches you sir when it came to League Championship play. I have always felt that this was one achievment of yours that has been overlooked.

I wondered if you could tell me something about the Dodger 'tradition'. Why was it different or special to be a Dodger?

Seth -
It was a pleasure to add to the history and tradition of the Dodgers -

Winning begets tradition and the Dodgers and Yankees probably have the most in that category - It is a simple equation -

fundamentals + talent + class + style = "Tradition & Excellence"

Good Luck.

Steve Garvey

April 12, 1996

SPARKY ANDERSON
Born 1934, Bridgewater, South Dakota. Manager, 1970–1995; Cincinnati Reds, Detroit Tigers. Anderson managed the Cincinnati "Big Red Machine" of the '70s to four pennants ('70, '72, '75, '76) and two World Championships ('75, '76). As the Detroit Tigers' pilot, he won another World Series in 1984—the only manager ever to win it in both leagues. His more than 2000 career victories rank him the fifth-winningest manager of all time.

Dear Mr. Anderson:

I wondered how you would rate the fabled "Big Red Machine" Reds that you managed in the 70's in baseball history? Also, did you have a favorite player on that team?

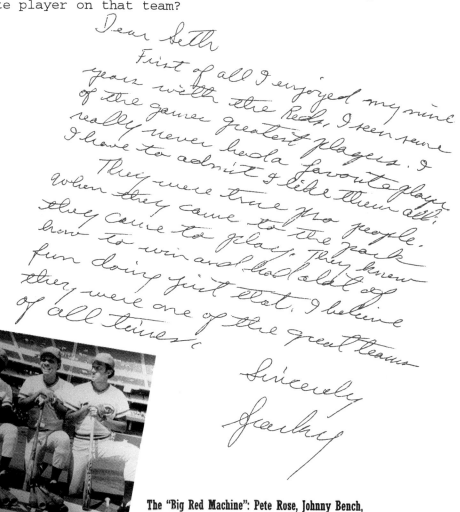

Dear Seth

First of all I enjoyed my nine years with the Reds. I seen some of the games greatest players. I really never hada favorite player. I have to admit I like them all.

They were true pro people. When they came to the park they came to play. They knew how to win and had alot of fun doing just that. I believe they were one of the great teams of all times.

Sincerely

Sparky

The "Big Red Machine": Pete Rose, Johnny Bench, Joe Morgan, Tony Perez, and Davy Concepcion

GEORGE CISAR
Born 1912, Chicago, Illinois.
Outfielder, 1937; Brooklyn
Dodgers. In 20 games with
the Dodgers, he rapped six
singles in 29 at-bats for a
.207 batting average. I wondered if the Brooklyn players
rode with the fans by sub-
way to the games and what
the players of the '30s did
before their games.

Dear Seth: 8-21-95

Received your letter and was glad to hear from an older era fan

Yes we did ride to the ball-park (Ebbetts Field) with the fans (by El mostly) and occasionally by cab when we were late and they were a great bunch and I'll never forget it.

We spent our free time mostly going to movies or just killing time walking around town and visiting. (There was no TV then in the 1930s you know.)

Yes its a new ball-game now Seth, and I hope they didn't screw it up with the past strike. Lets hope not but I think baseball won't be the same for quite awhile.

Sincerely,
George Cisar

P.S. The flavor of the game has improved to my estimation, conditions and ball-parks are better but there could be some improvements on attitudes for all concerned.

P.S.S. Good Luck to you.

135

October 12, 1995

Dear Mr. Neccai:

A few months ago, you signed a baseball for me. Thank you very
much--it looks great! I had you write on the ball what I consider
to be an amazing feat that you had accomplished--striking out 27
batters in a no hitter you threw in a minor-league game in 1952
before getting called up to the Pirates. I wondered if you could
tell me how you did it? Also, did that give you a "reputation" of
being unhittable going into the big leagues?

10-17-95

Seth,

Striking out 27 gave some fans false hope that
I could continue to strike out great numbers of
batters. That was a one time event in the history
of professional baseball. It gets tougher as the class
gets higher & did for me. No one in the big league
feared me. Control was my problem and an
arm injury in spring of 53 ended my very short
career. It was great while it lasted.

Best Wishes
Ron Necciai

DAVE PHILLEY
Born 1920, Paris, Texas. Outfielder, 1941, 1946–1962; Chicago White Sox and seven other teams. The switch-hitter was one of the great pinch-hitters of all time, with eight in a row to end the 1958 season, and then a ninth straight pinch hit at the start of the '59 season—a new major league record. In 1961 he set the single-season American League record for pinch hits with 24.

February 22, 1995

Dear Mr. Philley:

I always thought that your achievement of 9 consecutive pinch-hits in 1959 was fantastic as was your 24 pinch singles in '61. I wonder if you could you tell me something about the 'art' of pinch-hitting? It seems like a much more difficult discipline.

I think the art of Pinch hitting is oberservation, Watching Pitchers in Situations like you would be hitting. Looking for a certain pitch. Some Pitches I could Cale myself some Pitchers gave their Pitches away by doing thing different on Pitches

Dave Philley

FRENCHY BORDAGARAY

Born 1910, Coalinga, California. Outfielder and third baseman, 1934–1945; Brooklyn Dodgers, St. Louis Cardinals, and three other teams. His fun-loving exploits are part of baseball lore. Once, when he was running for a fly ball in the outfield, his hat fell off and he chased the hat—not the ball! His .312 batting average as a pinch hitter is the second highest of all time.

Pepper Martin's Mudcat Band: Lon Warneke, Frenchy Bordagaray, Bob Weiland, Pepper Martin, Bill McGee

February 6, 1995

Dear Mr. Bordagaray:

A few months back you answered my letter asking you
how you got your nickname etc.I really appreciated
your response.

Since your response I've read a lot about you. I
didn't know you were so colorful during your playing
days. The story of you running after your hat instead
of a fly ball is hilarious--is it true? What were some
of your funniest moments?

I PLAYED THE VIOLIN IN THE HIGH
SCHOOL ORCHESTRA. ALSO IN THE
COLLEGE ORCHESTRA. I ALSO PLAYED A
WASH BOARD IN PEPPER MARTINS
MUDCAT BAND.
    MY FAMILY HAD 8 CHILDREN
AND THEY ALL PLAYED AN INSTRUMENT
                    "Frenchy"

January 23, 1995

Dear Mr. Labine:

I am a 34 year-old songwriter living in Los Angeles. I
was always amazed that you pitched two of your most
incredible games before and after two 'historic'
contests; You beat Turley 1-0 after Larsen's perfect
game in the '56 World Series and you beat Branca the
game before Thomson's 'shot heard 'round the world.'
Incredible!

I know your time is very valuable, but I wondered if
you could tell me (below) what was the most nervous
you ever were on the mound--who were you facing and
what was the circumstance? I truly would be fascinated
by your response sir.

In answer to the above questions —

*In the 2nd game of the 1951 playoffs against
the N.Y Giants at the Polo Grounds.*

*I had the bases loaded in the early innings
with a 0-0 tie score and Bobby Thomson at the
plate. Fortunately, we did get him out but
I was extremely nervous.*

Thanks for asking —

Clem Labine

141

JOE RUDI
Born 1946, Modesto, California. Oufielder, 1967–1982; K.C./ Oakland A's, California Angels, and Boston Red Sox. Very steady at the plate and in the field, he will always be remembered for his fabulous catch against the outfield wall in the 1972 World Series against Cincinnati. He was a major cog in the Oakland A's machine that churned out three straight World Series championships from 1972 to 1974. I wondered what he learned from his coach in Oakland in the late '60s, Joe DiMaggio, and what he missed most about baseball.

From the desk of . .
Joe Rudi

Dear Seth,

Thank you for your nice letter. My time with the A's during those years was a tremendous experience. We had a great time, nothing like being on a winning team. Joe DiMaggio was my idol. He taught me alot about playing the outfield. I miss all the guys the most, we sort of grew up together. We never did receive the credit for being a great team. God Bless Joe

June 16, 1995

Dear Mr. Knowles:

I am a 34 year-old songwriter living in Los Angeles. I know your time is very valuable, but I wondered if you could tell me (below) what it was like to pitch in every game of a seven game World Series as you did in 1973? Was it exciting? I would truly appreciate your response sir.

I've enclosed a self-addressed, stamped envelope if you decide to jot down a note or two. Again, thank you for your time.

Sincerely,

Seth Swirsky

It's THE GREATEST memory I have other than my KIDS.

Darold Knowles

144

December 24, 1994

Dear Mr. Rhodes:

I wondered what the Giant bench was like after you hit
that home run in the 10th inning of the first game of
the '54 Series. Do you think your hit made everyone on
the team believe you could knock off the powerful Indians?

Dear Seth,
Leo Durocher had us so fired up We could have
beat The 1927 Yankees—
Dusty Rhodes

145

January 20, 1995

Dear Mr. Cowan:

I'll never forget the game in which the Yankees traded you in the
middle of a double-header to the Angels. Didn't you play game one
with the Yanks and game two with the Angels?   How bizarre!

I wonder if you could tell me what that was like?

Seth —
      I was actually traded after the game
on the final nite of a series at Anaheim Stadium
right after the all star break. I just moved
my equipment & bags from the visitors clubhouse
to the home teams — felt great as I was coming home
to Calif. My $16,000 salary & 2 kids made living
in N.Y. City very difficult (not much easier in Calif)

146

April 2, 1995

Dear Mr. Hemus:

I wondered if you could tell me what it was like to play with and manage Stan Musial? I never got to see him play as I was born after his great years. I truly would be interested if you would tell me what made him so great.

Dear Seth,

Playing with Stan Musial with all of his great ability, along with his dedication helped make me a better player. I talked to him numerous times to try and gain an insight in why he was such a great hitter and all around ball player – The information I gained from him was that you had to dedicate your every effort on concentrating on the pitcher, his every move, his best pitch and what to expect in a given situation. The thing he stressed most was concentration. To manage him was like a piece of cake. Every one respected him and he would talk to the players. "over"

147

"The Man" and "The Manager"

with the manager's best interest at heart. He instilled in the players that team work was the key to success. He led by his approach to the game. He was never real high or not low which helped the other ball players.

Best wishes

Solly Hemus

February 27, 1995

WHITEY LOCKMAN
Born 1926, Lowell, North Carolina. First baseman, outfielder, 1945, 1947–1960; New York Giants and three other teams. His clutch double in the ninth inning of the playoff game with the Dodgers kept the furious Giant rally alive, setting the table for Bobby Thomson's heroics.

Dear Mr. Lockman:

I thought your double in the ninth inning of the 3rd playoff game against the Dodgers in '51 was one of the all-time clutch hits. I know your time is very valuable, but I wondered if you could tell me what Bobby Thomsen's home run looked like to you from your perspective at second base? How did you experience the home run and was it your happiest moment in baseball?

Hi Seth,

Thanks for the compliment. It was a big hit but Bobby's was even bigger. When he hit the pitch from Branca, I knew we were at least tied. And as the ball soared towards left field, I felt it may leave the park. But then it began to sink and barely got into the seats. After crossing home plate I tried to lift Bobby onto my shoulders after he came in but too many people were jumping on him so all I got for my trouble was a stiff neck. It was a great feeling to finally be on a pennant winner and to have accomplished it in that manner was the ultimate satisfaction. Of course we had many tedious games during the last 47 game of the '51 season. We won 39 of them. A great and exciting time.

Sincerly,
Whitey Lockman

Lockman, #25, trying to hoist Bobby Thomson onto his shoulders

February 22, 1995

Dear Mr. Abrams:

I have a ball that is signed by the 1951 Dodgers.

I know your time is very valuable, but I wondered if
you could tell me something about that team. Was it
tougher to lose to the Giants in the playoffs that
year or to the Yankees in World Series past?

Dear Seth

Ralph Branca found out that their park was wired all the way to the scoreboard. They were getting our signs in the binoculars. All year long they never used it because they won their share of games. When they went way behind the Dodgers, they started stealing signs. It's easy to hit a fast ball, or curve when you know its coming! We would have beaten the Yankes had we won! Goodluck and may you write many song hits!

Sincerely Cal Abrams

could tell me what is your fondest memory of

August 24, 1995

Dear Mr. Scheib:

You were the sixth youngest player to ever play in the majors. When you pitched for the Philadelphia A's on September 6th, 1943, you were only 16 years and 8 months old.

I wondered if you could tell me if your family came to see you pitch that day and whether you were nervous before the game? Did your dad or mom have any words of advice?

I am the Youngest ever to Play in the American League. one Person in Nat. League was Younger.

In Answer to Your Questions, Yes my Parent were there when in Pitched in my first Game, in fact my Parents also had to sign the Contract, And since I signed & was in my first Game, it all happened in the Same day.

(over)

CARL SCHEIB
Born 1927, Gratz, Pennsylvania.
Righthanded pitcher, 1943–
1945, 1947–1954; mostly with
the Philadelphia Athletics. Of
the 14,000 players ever to
wear a major league uniform,
he was among the youngest
when he broke in.

I was not too nervous the first time, because I had been with the team for several month, & had gotten used to the Crowd & Games, although it was a very big thrill

Carl Scheib

July 21, 1995

Dear Mr. Caballero:

I was looking through the record books the other day, and I noticed that you were one of the youngest ever to play in big league ball -- 16 years old when you played 4 games with the Phillies in 1944. I think that is amazing!

I wondered if you could tell me if you were nervous the first time you took your position at third base? Also, was there anyone on the team who took you under his wing?

I am the youngest player ever to play 3rd base in the major league 16 Yr old.... An been nervous when game started. I was O.K.— before game I had butterflies. It was an incredible experience. I was playing American Legion ball one week, the next week I was playing in the Major Leagues. Freddie Fitzsimmons my first manager took me under his wing & told me to play like he know I could.

(over) Ralph "Putsy" Caballero Best wishes

P.S. Send me a song about baseball when you write one.

154

11/7/95

Bob Johnson and Roy Johnson were half brothers.
At the time, Bob played left field for the Philadelphia Athletics
and Roy left field for the Boston Red Sox. It was a night
game in the A's ball park during the summer of '37 or '38.

Bob Johnson, playing left, noted a couple of bats
(nocturnal mammals) cohabiting while affixed to the bleacher
wall. He removed them from the wall and placed them
under Roy's glove. Gloves were left in the field in those
days.

When the inning was over and Roy Johnson went
to pick up his glove, the bats, now disengaged,
flew up in Roy's face. An excitable guy, he dropped
his glove and took off as fast as the bats.

The players on the A's particularly enjoyed
this one.

Bill Werber

155

BOBBY DOERR
Born 1918, Los Angeles,
California. Second baseman,
1937–1944, 1946–1951; Boston
Red Sox. Hall of Fame, 1986. A
quiet leader on the field, he hit
223 home runs and knocked in
more than 100 runs six times.
An eight-time All Star, he never
played a position other than
second base once during his
entire 14-year career.

March 5, 1995

Dear Mr. Doerr:

Was there ever a time that you stood at your second base position in front of a full Fenway crowd on a beautiful summer day and felt a rush of happiness that you were where you were at that moment in your life?

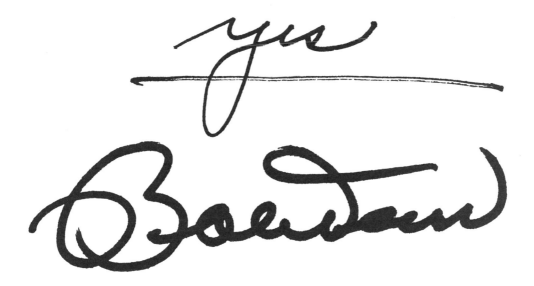

DON GUTTERIDGE
Born 1912, Pittsburg, Kansas. Second baseman, 1936–1940, 1942–1948; mostly with the St. Louis Cardinals and St. Louis Browns. He played on three of baseball's most fabled teams: the "Gas House Gang" Cardinals of the '30s, the A.L. champion '44 St. Louis Browns, and the mighty '46 Boston Red Sox, led by Ted Williams.

December 12, 1994

Dear Mr. Gutteridge:

I am a 34 year-old songwriter living in Los Angeles. I
know your time is very valuable but I wondered if you
could answer two questions for me (at the bottom or on
the back perhaps). Was it more fun to be in the world
series on the 44 Browns or the 46 Red Sox? Also, what
made that Red Sox team so special in your opinion?

I've enclosed a self-addressed, stamped envelope for
your convenience if you decide to answer. I very much
appreciate your time sir and thank you.

Sincerely,

[signature]

Seth Swirsky

Dear Seth:

First of all playing in a World Series is a lot of fun and
and a lot of satisfaction. You realize that you have accomplished a
goal.

1944 was my first World Series and I truly enjoyed every minute
of it even tho were did not win it all. I suppose I enjoyed it more
because I felt that I contributed more to winning the pennent, I felt
I had a big part in it,

But the 1946 was really great too because I was playing with
great Hall OF FAMERS. Altho I was just a utility player.

I had fun and enjoyed both Series. and I enjoyed being in 1959
Series against Dodgers altho I was only a coach. I felt that I contribute
something that year too.

Thank you for remembering Don Gutteridge

Transcripts

Woody English (pp. 2–3)
Seth—Babe Ruth did <u>not</u> call his H.R. I was playing 3rd base that game and he held two fingers up indicating two strike[s]—The press indicated he pointed which he did <u>not</u>—He never said he called it. When asked he replyed the papers said I <u>did</u>.

The Cub bench never let up on him.

Woody English

Cal Ripken, Jr. (pp. 4–5)
Dec. 21, 1995

Dear Seth,

When I was small, I remember competing with my sister and brothers for time with my dad. Baseball occupied a lot of my dad's time, but he spent as much time as he could with us kids.

On Saturday mornings, my dad conducted a baseball clinic for the Orioles. I quickly figured out that because my sister and my brothers weren't interested in a boring baseball clinic, I could go with my dad and get some time alone with him.

The hours in the car spent with my dad driving to and from the ballpark on Saturday mornings still remains one of my most vivid—and favorite—childhood memories.

Sincerely,

Cal

Don Larsen (pp. 6–7)
Every pitcher knows when the first hit happens. I figured there was a chance after the 7th inning, but facing the Dodgers of that era you knew that anything could happen.

I was very nervous in the 9th but conscious of the fact that this was a big game and that I had eight great players behind me.

DL

Bob Cain (pp. 8–9)
Bob Swift and I did talk about pitching to Eddie and Bob wanted to lay down to give me a low target, but Ed Hurley, the umpire, said no. None of us knew anything about Eddie coming to bat. The main thing is that we won the game 6-2.

Bob Cain

Enos Slaughter (pp. 10–11)
(See p. 10 for typewritten letter)

Warren "Bill" Peace (p. 12)
1/4/96

Dear Mr. Swirsky,

I received your letter and thanks for the donation. Yes we had quite a few white fans at our games especially when we played in the major leagues parks.

No we never had any resentment toward the white teams. But there was one minor league team in Brooklyn that pulled some dirty tricks on us in order to beat us. They would freeze one set of balls over nite for us to hit and their white umpires gave us the regular balls to pitch to them. They could hit the balls out of the park, and we couldn't hit the frosen balls out of the infield. We never knew they were doing this until after our league folded.

Hope I answered your questions,

Yours Truly

Bill Peace

Carl Erskine (p. 13)
2/26/95

Hi Seth—

The most nervous I ever was on a baseball field was Dodger Stadium—July, 1992 when I played the Canadian & American National Anthem before a Montreal/Dodger game—on my harmonica—45,000 attendance. (I really enjoy music)—(no mistakes)

Actually I was always keyed up before I pitched but truly never nervous.—As close as I ever came however was my rookie year when I was called in to pitch in Pitts—bases loaded to face Ralph Kiner.—The crowd was going crazy for Kiner to hit a grand slam. I did not disappoint that big Pitts. crowd.—

Regards,

Carl Erskine

Ted Williams (pp. 14–15)
Best advise was from Rogers Hornsby

"get a good ball to hit"

Ted Williams

Carroll Hardy (pp. 16–17)

In August 1960, Ted's last year, Ted fouled a pitch off the foot. It hurt him so much that he had to leave the game. I was called to finish his at bat. No one thought a thing about it at the time. It wasn't until Ted finished the 1960 season and all his statistics were finalized that they realized that the time I finished his at bat was the only time anyone ever pinch hit for Ted.

Carroll Hardy
The only man to pinch hit for Ted Williams

Dave Stapleton (pp. 18–19)

Seth,

Yes, I was surprised because I had already loosened up my legs and arm to go into the game in the 7th inning. I had usually gone in at this time in all other play-off games we were ahead. The reason he left Buckner in was to be in the field when we won the game so he could celebrate with the others. As you well know, nobody got to celebrate because of this bad decision. Mr. McNamara never had my respect as a manager or person but that doesn't matter. It does no good to beat a dead dog. He has to live with his decision the rest of his life.

And great Red Sox fans all over the country have to continue to suffer on as a result of it. And I feel sometimes that I got released after the "86" season because he didn't want me there to remind him of his mistake. I have talked to hundreds & hundreds of fans in the past years but none by mail. I hope this helps you understand.

Sincerely,
Dave Stapleton

John McNamara (pp. 20–21)

Seth:

Sorry for the delay in returning your letter. I guess the answer to your question was 1st, talent. We put a team concept as our priority, which I tried to do every place that I managed. It was fun & I tried to dismiss my media critics because they have never shared what I lived & enjoyed. Thank you for your kind message.

Sincerely
John McNamara

Harmon Killebrew (pp. 22–23)

8-29-95

Dear Seth,

Please forgive the long delay in answering your letter! I even took it to Japan with me in hopes that I would get it answered!

In answer to your question about my father—he passed away when I was 16 and never got to see me play Major League baseball. But, he was the biggest influence on my athletic career. He got me started playing all sports at a very early age. You may have heard my Hall of Fame acceptance speech when I told how my mother was complaining to my Dad about the holes in the yard and he told her we weren't raising grass—we're raising boys!

Sincerely,
Harmon Killebrew

Phil Niekro (pp. 24–25)

Its a longer story than I can write on this paper. My greatest game for me was when I won my 300th game in 1985 while pitching with the Yankees, winning the game 9-0 while my father was on his death bed. It took me 5 games to finally win it, how he held on that long I will never know. Someday maybe I can tell you the whole story about it. It is truly a movie waiting to be put together. (Hopefully.)

Sincerely,
Phil Niekro

Dolph Camilli (pp. 26–27)

More fun and less money
Brooklyn Dodgers
Dolph Camilli

Al Gionfriddo (pp. 28–29)

It was great to play in the 40's. We did not make much money but we play hard because it was a job and we play for our fans. They knew all the players by first names.
Al Gionfriddo

Bobby Thomson (pp. 30–31)

Hello Seth, Nice to hear from you. I admired Joe DiMaggio because he played the game with dignity and grace. I admired Ted Williams for his batting prowess. I played against Joe in the 1951 Series and I played with Ted at Boston in 1960.

I have been by myself a few times in my life when the Home run was shown. It's a bit of a thrill by myself more so than when I'm with a group.

Best Regards,
Bobby Thomson

Andy Pafko (pp. 32–33)

1/26/95
Dear Seth,

Received your letter in regards to Bobby Thomson's "shot heard around the world." At first I thought I would have a chance at it because it was a line drive. But instead of a sinking line drive, it took off. It would be an out in Ebetts Field but the Polo Grounds it was a home run.

To me it was one of the biggest disappointments of my major league career. A few years later I am a member of the Braves when Thomson is traded to the Braves, and now we are team mates. Not only did he become a team mate but my room mate. I asked him how he felt after he hit the famous home run and his answer was thats history, did not want to talk about it. He showed me a lot of class. To this day—I tell people—if anyone hit that home run, I am glad it was Bobby Thomson. At least I am part of history—watching the home run with me watching it go over my head. I am often asked about it. But at the time it was a big big disappointment.

Regards—
Andy Pafko—

Billy Johnson (pp. 34–35)

at the start of the 51 season I had #7 and Mickey wanted that #7 badly. I said OK it didn't make any difference to me so I took #24 that's all that was to it.
Bill

Richie Scheinblum (p. 36)

(See p. 36 for typewritten letter)

Tim McClelland (p. 37)

Seth,

I wasn't scared because Brett was charging out at a man who stands 6'6" tall, weighs 250 pounds, had protective equipment on, and had a bat in his hand—George wasn't very smart! We are happy with our call because we went by the rule book and called what we had to do.

Thanks for writing. It is nice to hear from people concerning umpiring.

Sincerely,
Tim McClelland
A.L. #36

Ken Brett (pp. 38–39)

1—I was 17 when leaving to play pro ball. George was 12. Hard for me to notice his ability. My father always thought he would be the better hitter. When he reached the majors—we were in opposite leagues. . . . I never saw him play . . . but friends told me he was going to be special.

2—He hit about .300 off me careerwise. And I wanted beat him very bad—
KB

Rick Ferrell (pp. 40–41)

I have been asked that question many times—I always answer by saying—

The greatest left hand pitcher I ever caught was Lefty Grove—The greatest right hander I ever caught was my brother Wes Ferrell.
Rick Ferrell

Al Downing (pp. 42–43)

February 18, 1995
Dear Mr. Swirsky,

In reference to your letter inquiring of my friendship with Henry Aaron prior to, and after April 8th, 1974, I find that to be the most interesting question I've been asked relative to that event. I knew Mr. Aaron only as a fellow Major League Baseball player, both before, and after, the event, and contrary to media reporting, most professional athletes are acquaintances, involved in the same field of endeavor, not "soul buddies," as is often depicted.

Best Always,
Al Downing

Duke Snider (pp. 44–45)

It proved to all fans and to us that we were as good of a team as the Yankees. Not better but as good!
Duke

Johnny Podres (pp. 46–49)

The Dodgers of 55 had many veteran players who knew how to play, they were embarrassed by the Yankees many times and I as a young pitcher was very thrilled to be a Dodger and thanks to Sandy Amoros for the Great Catch in the 7th game.
Best Wishes
Johnny Podres

Johnny Pesky (pp. 50–51)

My all time All Star Team.
1B—Jimmie Foxx, 2B—Bobby Doerr, SS—Joe Cronin,
3B—Frank Malzone or Wade Boggs
C—Carlton Fisk, Birdie Tebbetts [sic]
OF—Williams, Rice, Yastremski, Lynn, Evans
RHP—Clemons, Kinder, LHR Radatz, LHP Parnell, Hurst
Johnny Pesky

Sal Durante (pp. 52–53)

Thinking back to the day I caught the ball, the excitement was overwhelming.

I can still see the baseball in flight. Hoping, I would be the one to catch it.

When I met Roger, the only thing I wanted to do, was to give him the baseball. He said, keep it and make some money. I'll never forget what a great guy he was.
Sincerly,
Sal Durante

Ralph Houk (p. 54)

Dear Seth

In regards to the question you asked me about Roger Maris's 61st home run:

Every one on the team was pulling for Roger to get it. The quicker the better as we were looking forward to the World Series. I remember Mantle telling me "I hope he gets it today.

Of course every one in the dugout was excited and glad it was over so we could look forward to the World Series.

As manager of the team, I was happy because now the press would let him alone—he had been through a lot the previous weeks.
My Best Regards,
Ralph Houk,
Mgr. 61 N.Y. Yankees

Cal McLish (p. 55)

Dear Seth

Received your letter requesting info. on how my name originated. The only thing I was ever told (by my mother) that of 6 previous children my dad was not involved in naming any of them—so he supposedly tried to catch up, using me. He named me after a president, a Roman emperor and an indian chief. Being part indian I guess he felt he had to get an indian name in there some where—i've always claimed he had to be in the firewater to give a kid a name like that. Calvin Coolidge was president when I was born (1925) Don't know where Julius Caesar came from. That's about all I know. I was called Buster by all my family.
Regards,
Cal

Elden Auker (pp. 56–57)

In the 6 years, Hank & I were playing for the Tigers, only one incident occured when his Jewish Heritage was ever noted. This happened in about 1937 when we were playing the Chicago White Sox in Detroit. Only Hank heard the remark after he grounded out & was returning to our dugout. Evidently, someone of the White Sox, called from the Bench, to Hank back "You Yellow Jew S—B—." Following the game, Hank walked into the White Sox Clubhouse & said "the man that called me a "Yellow Jew S—B—", stand up—nobody stood up! That was the end. The only time in 6 years, I ever saw or heard any slurring remarks about Hank Greenberg. I hasten to add, the man that made the remark was the smartest player on the White Sox Club—Hank could & would have wiped up the clubhouse floor with him.
Elden Auker

Al Rosen (p. 58)

Outside of our few years together, Hank and I didn't see much of each other. As an aspiring young player, I admired his exploits and chose him as my "idol." We rarely discussed Anti-Semitism as it applied to our careers. Undoubtedly it existed, but our bent in life was to let our success disarm any overt prejudice.

With regards,

Al Rosen

Ned Garver (p. 59)

Seth—

Bill Veeck was in a class by himself. Had more good promotional ideas every day than most owners had in their lifetime. He loved baseball & would do nothing to hurt it. Not the case today. Sad-sad-sad. He might trade you tomorrow but when you played for him, he made you feel 10' tall.

The thing I remember about Grandstand Managers nite was in the 1st inning—runs in—still men on 1st & 3rd— only one out & they voted to bring the infielder in. Sherm Lollar—my catcher— came out to me and stalled until Zack Taylor [the Browns' manager] finally got an "infield back" vote. I then got a ground ball for a double play to end the inning.

Ned

Albie Pearson (pp. 62–63)

Dear Seth—

I didn't have the pleasure of meeting "Ike" until 1962 when I was with the Angels. We were training in Palm Springs near his home, the El Dorado CC in Indian Wells. He became a "real" Angel fan, attending many "Spring" games.

In 1963 I had the pleasure of playing a little golf and presenting him a silver bat as the Angels "#1 fan."

He was a very gracious and special person.

Personal regards to you Seth and God bless you Isiah 9:6

Albie Pearson

Bob Stevens (pp. 64–65)

In my day (1925–1934) baseball underwent a big change.

Night baseball crept in slowly. The lights were terrible in the beginning. Nothing, really, can take the place of the sun. Gloves were smaller in my day, travel was by train in the AA leagues and the 'big' leagues. At Newark in the Int. League (AA), we had two Pullmans; at Phila (Nat'l League) we had one Pullman. Good luck.

Bob Stevens

Phils 1931

Dick Williams (pp. 66–67)

The 1967 Red Sox were a young group of players who never experienced winning before and what it took to reach that goal—I was very hard and demanding on the players and at times we had very strained relations but they found out it took hard work plus the talent to be succesful [sic]. Replacing Conigliaro was very hard and seven (7) different players played there after he went down. His talent was special!

D.W.

Jim Lonborg (p. 68)

Dear Seth,

I wasn't actually nervous before the seventh game. I had faced the Cardinals twice in games 2 & 5 and beat them. I was actually more fatigued than nervous and was hoping we'd score some early runs off Bob Gibson.

I spent more time with my catcher before the game to develop strategy. We knew how to get the hitters out. We just didn't know how my arm would feel after only two days rest.

Jim Lonborg

Nelson Briles (p. 69)

Seth—

Happy Birthday! I am Director of Corporate Relations with the Pirates so I'm still involved with major league baseball. As to your question about Northrup's line drive triple in game seven of the '68 World Series—I thought Curt Flood was going to catch the ball until he slipped trying to go back on the ball. My heart sank as I then realized we were not going to repeat as World Champions. Life goes on!! Have a glass of wine for me!

Nellie Briles

Tot Presnell (p. 70)

don't believe Babe ever wanted to be a manger [sic]. He would never be a manager, cause he could not remember signs. He never had one sign to remeber [sic]. Couldn't remember names. Everyone knows Babe was a hard drinker, you might call him a lone wolf. Away from the park, we never saw him.

Paul Hopkins (p. 71)

5/12/95

Dear Seth,

Re—59th H.R. to Babe Ruth (1927), my 1st appearance in major's with 2 out, bases loaded, 2 & 3 on hitter & then the baseball lands in 4 or 5th row. After inning over on way to bench my eyes were a bit wet.

Joe Hauser (pp. 74–75)

Dear Seth:

#1, I broke the Babe's record of 61 home runs 2 times already, I got 63 homers at Baltimore International League, and 69 homers at Minneapolis in 1933— American Association both teams were playing Triple A baseball next to the Big Leagues. surprising you to ask me to break Ruths record of 61 homers. I done broke his record 2 times once in 1930 & the other time in 1933 at Minneapolis, 1930 at Baltimore, surprising you ask a question of that was broken over 50 yrs. ago. Baseball is always fun minor or Major League hope you are satisfied or my answer.

Kindest Regards,

Joe Hauser

Mrs. Jack Wilson (p. 76)

(See p. 76 for typewritten letter)

Gerry Staley (p. 77)

don't charge for autographs. I feel honored to be asked. I'm just thankful to be alive and able to do it.

Gerry Staley

Jim Kaat (pp. 78–79)

1/29/95

Seth,

He saw me pitch Game 2 of the 1965 World Series. We beat Sandy Koufax and the Dodgers that day 5-1. I was not any more nervous than any other game. It was a great Father-Son "feeling" because he was such a baseball fan.

Sincerely,

Jim Kaat

Whitey Ford (pp. 80–81)

Dec 5, 1995

Dear Seth

When I was 10 yrs. old, I went to see Joe Di Maggio at Yankee Stadium for the first time. Little did I think that eleven yrs. later he would be playing centerfield for me in my first start at a Yankee in 1950.

I was so in awe of him, that it was many years later before I felt comfortable have a chat with him.

He was one of the greatest!

All the best

Whitey Ford

Al Milnar (pp. 82–83)

Joe DiMaggio

Pitching to one of the great hitters in bascball in a way makes me proud of my luck againest [sic] Joe DiMaggio in his amazing streak of 56 games in a row I can't say in truth I remember the hits Joe got in the streak in 1941— June 16 he had 1 for 4 June 23 he hit 1- for 5 a double July 16 he hit 2 for 3. His no. 56 was a ground ball hit in front of the batters box hit hard with over spin to my right and Boudreau's left he came close to catching it. He had to play Joe to pull me and we missed by a step or two. Joe had 4 hits for 11 off me. He hit 408 in his streak. He was stopped by Al Smith and Jim Bagby Jr. There were two great plays by Ken Kelkner [sic] and Lou Boudreau to end it. Joe had 15 more games in a row after no. 56. I can't see how it will ever be broken

Cliff Mapes (pp. 84–85)

Dear Seth:

As you can see by my autograph I no longer handle a pen well. So my wife is my "write arm." My tho'hts, her pen.

Playing for the Yankees is a feeling that can't be told. Only those of us who have been fortunate enough to do it can know the wonder of it. I know the game & the players have changed—remember I was there almost 50 years ago. And my locker was next to Joe Di Maggio. I was given my idols #3 to wear—talk about "in awe of." I'm not saying all the guys were "saints" but there was a team spirit, family atmosphere, all professionals—Di Magg could get his point across with just with a look. He played his heart out & expected the same of everyone else. Charlie Keller was a wonderful example of what a man could & should be. Our pitchers, the late Raschi (my roomie) Reynolds (my good friend & Lopat were wonderful—All were "Stars" but they were part of the team just like everyone else. As for a man in a clutch—Tom Henrich [sic] was it. If you needed a hit you called on Tommy—Seems like no matter who was called on—they could do the job—Those were wonderful years & I'm so grateful I shared them—The memories keep me going—

As for your being a songwriter—I can't imagine how you do what you do. I love music—Not all of it—but my cupboard is full of 40'-50' & a little 60s type. My wife likes the words—I'll take the instrumentals—Hope your career as a songwriter will be fulfilling to you—
Sincerely—
Cliff

Ken Raffensberger (p. 86)
Hi Seth.,
You better bet my parents were at the game, along with my 4 brothers, as Pittsburgh is only 200 miles from York.
I probably went along home with my parents, as we didn't play till Thurs. and Phila. is only 90 mile from York.
Kindest Regards,
Ken Raffensberger

Tom Underwood (p. 87)
I told him we would be on center stage tonight, throughout the country, not just in Toronto. So let's give them a show. Afterwards, I told him I was very proud of him. He's was & still is my best friend.
Tom Underwood

Al Kaline (pp. 88–89)
High—was to play on the world champion Detroit Tigers in '68. Also just to play in the Big Leagues for 22 years. Lowest disappointment—a lost on the last day of the season in 1967 and lose to Boston for the AL Championship.
Al Kaline

George Kell (pp. 90–91)
3/1/95
Dear Seth—
I first saw Brooks Robinson when I was traded to Baltimore—that was mid year 1956—He came to spring training in 1957—and I had been told he could handle the glove as well as any one—and boy could he ever—I don't think he even got a whole lot better with the glove—because he was picture perfect then.
He opened the season with us and played good—When a left hander pitched Brooks played third & I moved to first base—but he was young—swung at a lot of bad pitches—so about the All Star game Paul Richards sent him back to play every day—When he came back to stay two years later—he was a polished Major League Ball play—And of course went on to become a good clutch hitter—I did nothing to help him play [sic]—He was quoted once as saying I taught him how to act like a Major Leaguer—liked that very much—We remain great friends today—
Sincerely
George Kell

Brooks Robinson (pp. 92–93)
Dear Seth, Sorry this letter is so tardy, but put away with a few other things.
George Kell was one of two idols I had as a youngster growing up in Arkansas. I use to follow all of the big league players from Arkansas, knowing their stats and where they came from etc.
My rookie year 1957 was George Kell's last year. In fact, opening game in Washington D.C.'s Griffin Stadium, I played 3rd for the Orioles and George played first. George was a big influence in my life. George and his wife just kind of took me under their wing and

showed me what being a big leaguer was all about. In fact, he took me to my first stage play in New York.

Their has never been a more finer gentleman to put on a big league uniform than George. It was my good fortune to have him their in 1957 on the field and off. I tried to emulate him in many ways. And then the most exciting part was going into the Hall of Fame together in 1983. Could it get any better? A perfect ending.
Thanks
Brooks

Marty Marion (pp. 94–95)
Dear Seth—

To tell the truth—I don't know what I was thinking—?
Marty

Buddy Hassett (pp. 96–97)
Playing for the <u>Yankees</u> was by far the most fun because you were winning most of the time. <u>Brooklyn</u> had the best fans by far. <u>Boston</u> had the most polite and 2nd best fans
Buddy Hassett

Hobie Landrith (pp. 98–99)
Seth—

The Reds were playing the Giants that night and Leo Durocher would <u>not</u> let his catchers try to catch the ball after seeing the 1st ball dropped bury in the outfield grass. Yes, I tried it. I had a bet of free cokes with my team mates that I would touch one of the three attempts. I won the bet, but didn't catch one. The helicopter was lowered to 550 feet and I caught the 1st ball dropped. It felt like a sledge hammer hitting my mitt. It was fun. It was a real pecticle. All the best!
Hobie Landrith

Joe Ginsberg (pp. 100–101)
The story is true, I use it at outing's & dinner's, yes, I took a lot of heat from my team mates, but being a catcher, they know the peril's of the job, so they stop very fast.

Fred Lynn (pp. 102–103)
Dear Seth,

My favorite player was Willie Mays. I met him once, but we talked about golf & not baseball.

Best of luck with your songwriting.
Fred Lynn

Jerry Koosman (p. 104)
2/1/95
Dear Seth,

Since I pitched the last game of the '69 series, I was on the mound when Cleon caught the ball for the final out, & J. Grote was the 1st person I jumped on & hugged.
Sincerely
Jerry Koosman
P.S. Thanks for your nice letter.

Bud Harrelson (p. 105)
1/21/95
Dear Seth,

1969 was a wonderful season! Most of us seemed to move through that season as if we were dreaming. Why! Gil Hodges.

He was our inspiration and guide. He knew what he was doing and we followed. The games are well documented. All of us call recall incidences [sic] that we individually felt cause our success.

1969 was the legacy Gil Hodges left all of us.
#3
Buddy Harrelson

Art Smith (pp. 106–107)
From 1928 to 1933 I played professional ball, mostly minor league, with a brief stay with the White Sox in 1932. This was before the time of Jackie Robinson. From 1934 to 1941 I played with an all-white semi-pro team in the New York city area. We played 50% of our games with the teams in the Negro National League. They had players that should have been in the big leagues. Josh Gibson, Satchel Paige, Cool Papa Bell, Cannon ball Redding, Charleston, Thomas, Leonard (can't remember the first names.) I'm so glad they broke the color line years ago—because playing in the big leagues should be based on ability—not race. Did you see the Yankee–

Seattle series? Broke my heart—but the better team won. Yours in baseball—Art Smith

Virgil Trucks (p. 108)

My first major league game I pitched in Fenway Park in Boston. Johnny Pesky was the lead off hitter. On my first pitch he singled. Bobby Doerr the 2nd hitter hit my 1st pitch for a double. Ted Williams the 3rd hitter hit the first pitch I threw to him for a double. Steve O'Nial [*sic*] the manager for us called time, meeting me and the catcher Bob Swift at the mound. Steve never spoke to me, he said to Bob Swift the catcher, Say Bob, doesn't Virgil have it to-day. And Bob answered, how the hell do I know. I haven't caught a pitch yet, A true story. by,
Virgil Trucks

Jimmy Wynn (p. 109)

Dear Seth

My Greatest Moment in sports were my two years at Central State College, in Wilberforce, Ohio, and my signing of my professional Baseball contract with the Cincinnati Reds, and to see the tears come down my father's cheeks, that was the crowning moments of hard work and dedication for a future of baseball my "Desire."
Jim Wynn
Toy Cannon

Ferguson Jenkins (pp. 110–111)

1—My highest high was having 6 strike outs in an all-star game in Anaheim in 1967.
2—'91 Induction into the "Hall of Fame."
3—Winning 20 games 6 yrs. in a row for the Chicago Cubs.
4—Lowest part of my career was the trade from the Philly's in 1966. I was 21 yr. old.

Claude Osteen (p. 112)

I think my happiest moment in baseball was putting a Cincinnati Reds uniform on directly at the age of 17 out of high school and going straight to the M.L.

I've had many great moments; my first time wearing the Dodger uniform, 1st World Series start, win & shutout. It's very dificult to single one out.

Many times I've had the thoughts "a beautiful day, this is amazing" while standing on the mound at Dodger stadium.
Claude Osteen

Norm Sherry (p. 113)

In answer to your above question about what I saw that others hadn't, was nothing mechanical, I just sugested [*sic*] to him not to try to throw his fast as hard as he could. Instead of try to throw a 100 mph do it at 95. It made his control better.
Sandy was easy to catch as other pitchers did not have the great control he came to have—Also his F.B. was light with a little rise to it. Some pitchers have heavy F.B. and sinking action.
Norm Sherry

Bill Rigney (p. 114)

Seth—I was in the clubhouse—1st person I hugged was Horace Stoneham, the owner—
I had helped carry Don Mueller off the field in the 9th.
Best
Bill Rigney

Don Mueller (p. 115)

Friend Seth,
When I broke my ankle I was carried to the clubhouse, which was in center field. Lying on the training table, no radio, no one to talk to. I heard a roar; it could mean 1 of 2 things. Win or lose. And then the players came & were loud and laughing. Then I knew. My ankle had swollen the size of a football. But victory erased the pain.
My best to you friend
Don Mueller

Monte Irvin (pp. 116–117)

My greatest thrill was stealing home in the first inning of the 1951 World Series game against the Yankees.

My biggest disappointment was not winning the M.V.P. of the National League in 1951
Monte Irvin

Warren Spahn (p. 118)

I remember very well Mays first at bat. The information

we had was that he pulled away from the plate when he swung & that he couldn't reach the curve ball on the outside. The pitch he hit off me was a curve ball on the outside corner but from a left hander, he didn't pull away & thus the homerun.
Warren Spahn

Lucille Haefner (p. 119)

Dear Seth:—

Mickey passed away Jan 3/95. He suffered a stroke in Jan of 1989 and it left him totally helpless. He was in nursing home here in New Athens so I could be with him each day. I miss him very much but thank the Lord for taking him home—6 yrs was enough. He was a gentle man—good husband (58 yrs.) and wonderful father. Thank you for your interest in him—makes me happy to know so many remember him. He loved the game of baseball. Lucille (wife)

Richie Ashburn (pp. 120–121)

My mother and father were great "cheerleaders" during my youth—not only for me but also my brother and sisters.

My mother followed my career very closely—travelled and has always been close to my career accomplishments R.A.

Bob Feller (pp. 122–123)

Dear Seth:

Rogers Hornsby was my idol. I wanted to play 2nd base & did in American Legion Baseball before at age 15 pitched most of the time.

I pitched to Rogers Hornsby while he managed the St. Browns in 1936.

Sincerely Yours,
Bob Feller

Leo Nonnenkamp (pp. 124–125)

1/16/95

Dear Seth:—

So many changes in the game today. Equipment, playing fields, are so much better. Can't brag on the hours they play. Prefer our schedule—afternoon games, then an enjoyable dinner. More relaxing and less tension. Some better now, financially. Wouldn't be surprised, to read how that money is spent. Not much salary bargaining back then. Not so many teams in the Major Leagues, and so many more teams in the Minor league. So it was take what was offered, or.

Red Sox had quite a few established stars in '38. All were pretty friendly, but the extra players usually went our own way. "Lefty" Grove was at the end of his career—still he was real crafty. Foxx, Vosmik, Ben Chapman, Cramer—Higgens, Cronin all established stars, so they were never the rah-rah type. Maybe that is why Boston usually finished second to the Yankees. Bobby Doerr and Ted Williams were just breaking in—but didn't they both have outstanding careers?? Williams got all the attention, from all the players, when hitting, whether in a game or just batting practice. I would pick him as the best hitter, ever!!! Quite a thrill to <u>visit</u> all the parks, Yankee Stadium was super. Made you feel so small. Boston drew well there—quite a bit of rivalry between the teams. And so many of the better players, on both teams, Lou Gehrig, Ruth, Muesel, Ruffing, Gomez, Gordon, Rolfe and the best catcher in baseball—Bill Dickey.

Enjoyed my short stay, especially when Ben Chapman came up sickly- -that meant, I would have a chance to play. Would have been more to my liking, if I could have taken advantage of the opportunity.

Watch some T.V. games. We have a team here in LR, in the Texas League, sponsored by the St. L. Cardinals. Stay for about five innings—nite games get pretty late for this old-goat,
Sincerely
Leo

Bud Thomas (p. 126)

Ted Williams hit his first home run off me in April 1939, in Boston. Made me feel bad at the time, But after the years went own [sic], I dident [sic] feel so bad.
Good Luck
"Bud" Thomas

Bobby Shantz (p. 127)

Dear Seth,

Like I said, playing for the Yankees was the best 4 years of my baseball life. When pitching against the Yankees, I always thought I really done something special when I beat the powerful Yankees. In 1952 I beat them 4 times and one of those games was a 14 inning complete game in Yankee stadium. When it was all over that day, I really couldn't believe I pitched the whole game and beat them.

When I was traded to them in 1957, I felt like running all the way up to New York. Pitching for them was really great because I always knew I was going to get some runs and their defense was very good also. There was always a very good chance to get in the World Series also, which we did 3 of the 4 years I spent with them. A wonderful experience!! Also had the roommate of the century in Bobby Richardson. What a great guy!

Sincerely,
Bobby Shantz

Bobby Richardson (p. 128)

Just a note
Seth

To say thanks for your letter and especially the words about Mantle's funeral.

My dad did get to see me play on television for several years both Sat. games & World Series. I wish his health had allowed more than the 1 game that I played 3rd base.

Over the years the liner by McCovey seems to pick up speed and & a much more difficult play. That's true when you're looking back.

Thanks again—
Bobby Richardson

Billy Rogell (p. 129)

Dizzy Dean—<u>did</u> <u>not</u> <u>slide.</u> He came standing up and after he came to, first-thing he said <u>was</u> "did I brake [*sic*] up the double play?" He was lucky that I did not throw the ball as hard as I could. Frisch should of had his head examined why he let Dizzy run.

Ron Cey (pp. 130–131)

Hi Seth,

There was always a sense of responsibility to live up to the Dodger tradition. To try and stay on a level of past Dodger teams and players that became World Champions and Hall of Famers was an honor not a burden.

I believe we held our own by playing in four World Series and winning a World Championship in my ten years in Los Angeles.

Best Regards!
Ron Cey

Steve Garvey (p. 132)

Seth

It was a pleasure to add to the history and tradition of the Dodgers—Winning begets tradition and the Dodgers and Yankees probably have the most in that category—It is a simple equation: fundamentals + talent + class + style = "Tradition & Excellence".

Good Luck,
Steve Garvey

Sparky Anderson (p. 133)

Dear Seth

First of all I enjoyed my nine years with the Reds, I seen some of the games greatest players. I really never had a favorite player. I have to admit I like them all.

They were true pro people. When they came to the park they came to play. They knew how to win and had alot of fun doing just that. I believe they were one of the great teams of all times.

Sincerely
Sparky

George Cisar (pp. 134–135)

8/21/95
Dear Seth:

Received your letter and was glad to hear from an older era fan.

Yes we did ride to the ball-park (Ebbetts Field) with the fans (by El mostly) and occasionaly [*sic*] by cab when we were late and they were a great bunch and I'll never forget it.

We spent our free time mostly going to movies or just killing time walking around town and visiting. (There was no TV then in the 1930's you know.)

Yes its a new ball-game now Seth, and I hope they didn't screw it up with the past strike. Let's hope not but I think baseball won't be the same for quite awhile.

Sincerely,

George Cisar

P.S. The flavor of the game has improved to my estimation, conditions and ball-parks are better but there could be some improvements on attitudes for all concerned.

P.S.S. Good Luck to you.

Ron Necciai (p. 136)

10/17/95

Seth,

Striking out 27 gave some fans false hope that I could continue to strike out great numbers of batters. That was a one time event in the history of professional baseball. It gets tougher as the class gets higher & did for me. No one in the big league feared me. Control was my problem and an arm injury in spring of 53 ended my very short career. It was great while it lasted.

Best Wishes

Ron Necciai

Dave Philley (p. 137)

I think the art of pinch hitting is observation. Watching pitchers in situations like you would be hitting. Looking for a certain pitch. Some pitches I could call myself. Some pitchers gave their pitches away by doing things different on pitches.

Dave Philley

"Frenchy" Bordagaray (pp. 138–139)

I played the violin in the high school orchestra. Also in the college orchestra. I also playe a wash board in Pepper Martins Mudcat Band.

My family had 8 children and they all played an instrument

"Frenchy"

Clem Labine (pp. 140–141)

In answer to the above questions—In the 2nd game of the 1951 playoffs against the N.Y. Giants at the Polo Grounds.

I had the bases loaded in the early innings with a 0-0 tie score and Bobby Thomson at the plate. Fortunately, we did get him out but I was extremely nervous.

Thanks for asking—Clem Labine

Joe Rudi (pp. 142–143)

Dear Seth,

Thank you for your nice letter. My time with the A's during those years was a tremendous experience. We had a great time, nothing like being on a winning team. Joe DiMaggio was my idol. He taught me alot about playing the outfield. I miss all the guys the most, we sort of grew up together. We never did receive the credit for being a great team.

God Bless

Joe

Darold Knowles (p. 144)

It's the greatest memory I have other than my kids.

Darold Knowles

Dusty Rhodes (p. 145)

Dear Seth,

Leo Durocher had us so fired up we could have beat the 1927 Yankees—

Dusty Rhodes

Billy Cowan (p. 146)

Seth—

I was actually traded after the game on the final nite of a series at Anaheim Stadium right after the All Star break—I just moved my equipment & bags from the visitors clubhouse to the home teams—felt great as I was coming home to Calif. My $16,000 salary & 2 kids made living in N.Y. City very difficult (not much easier in Calif.)

Billy Cowan

Solly Hemus (pp. 147–148)

Dear Seth,

Playing with Stan Musial with, all of his great ability, along with his dedication helped make me a better player—

I talked to him numerous times to try and gain an insight in why he was such a great hitter and all around ball player— The information I gained from him was that you had to dedicate your every effort on concentrating on the pitcher, his every move, his best pitch and what to expect in a given situation. The thing he stressed most was concentration. To manage him was like a piece of cake—every one respected him and he would talk to the players with the managers best interests at heart. He instilled in the players that team work was the key to success. He led by his approach to the game. He was never real high or real low which helped the other players.
Best wishes
Solly Hemus

Whitey Lockman (p. 149)

Hi Seth,

Thanks for the compliment. It was a big hit but Bobby's was even bigger. When he hit the pitch from Branca, I knew we were at least tied. And as the ball soared towards left field, I felt it may leave the park. But then it began to sink and barely got into the seats. After crossing home plate I tried to lift Bobby onto my shoulders after he came in but too many people were jumping on him so all I got for my trouble was a stiff neck. It was a great feeling to finally be on a pennant winner and to have accomplished it in that manner was the ultimate satisfaction. Of course we had many tedious games during the last 47 game of the '51 season. We won 39 of them. A great and exciting time.
Sincerely,
Whitey Lockman
    P.S. Are you a lyricist?

Cal Abrams (p. 150)

Dear Seth

Ralph Branca found out that their park was wired all the way to the scoreboard. They were getting our signs with binoculars. All year long they never used it, because they won their share of games. When they went way behind the Dodgers, they started stealing signs. It's easy to hit a fastball, or curve, when you know its coming! We would have beaten the Yanks, had we won! Good luck and may you write many song hits!
Sincerely Cal Abrams

Elmer Klumpp (p. 151)

Dear Seth:

Yes Goose Goslin was a nice man, but a terrific competator [sic]. Enclosed are a couple of pictures, all I have left.

The favorite saying about a tough pitcher was, if the winning run was on base and his mother come up to pinch hit. he would knck her down on his first pitch.
Best wishes
Elmer Klumpp

Carl Scheib (pp. 152–153)

I am the youngest ever to play in the American League. One person in Nat. League was younger.

In answer to your questions, yes my parent were there when in pitched in my first game, in fact my parents also had to sign the contract, and since I signed & was in my first game, it all happened in the same day. I was not too nervous the first time, because I had been with the team for several months, & had gotten used to the crowd & games, although it was a very big thrill.
Carl Scheib

Putsy Caballero (p. 154)

am the <u>youngest player</u> ever to play 3rd base in the major league 16 yr old. . . . As been nervous when game started I was O.K . . . before game I had butterflies. It was an incredible experience. I was playing <u>American Legion</u> ball one week, the next week I was playing in the Major Leagues. <u>Freddie Fitzsimmons</u> my <u>first manager</u> took me under his wing & told me to play like he know I could.
Best Wishes,
Ralph "Putsy" Caballero

P.S. Send me a <u>song</u> about <u>baseball</u> when you write one.

Bill Werber (p. 155)
1/7/95

Bob Johnson and Roy Johnson were half brothers. At the time, Bob played left field for the Philadelphia Athletics and Roy left field for the Boston Red Sox. It was a night game in the A's ball park during the sumer of '37 or '38.

Bob Johnson, playing left, noted a couple of bats (nocturnal mammals) cohabiting while affixed to the bleacher wall. He removed them from the wall and placed them under Roy's glove. Gloves were left in the field in those days.

When the inning was over and Roy Johnson went to pick up his glove, the bats, now disengaged, flew up in Roy's face. An exciteable guy, he dropped his glove and took off as fast as the bats.

The players on the A's particularly enjoyed this one.
Bill Werber

Bobby Doerr (pp. 156–157)
<u>Yes</u>
Bob Doerr

Don Gutteridge (pp. 158–159)
(See p. 158 for typewritten letter)

Bibliography

The Baseball Encyclopedia. 9th ed. New York: Macmillan, 1993.

Blake, Mike. *Baseball Chronicles.* Cincinnati, Ohio: Betterway Books, 1994.

Dewey, Donald, and Nicholas Acocella. *The Biographical History of Baseball.*
New York: Carroll & Graf, 1995.

The Editors of the Sporting News. *Baseball.* New York: Galahad Books, 1993.

Nemec, David, and Peter Palmer. *Fascinating Baseball Facts.*
Lincolnwood, Ill.: Publications International, 1994.

Reichler, Joseph L. *The Great All-Time Baseball Record Book.* Rev. ed.
New York: Macmillan, 1993.

Acknowledgments

To my wife, Jody, whose love, support, and friendship can't be measured. And my son, Julian, whom the world revolves around. I love you.

For encouragement and assistance, heartfelt thanks to Darcy Ross, whose help on this project was invaluable; to Philip Turner, my editor; and to everyone at Kodansha America who helped shape this project and bring it to fruition.

Deep appreciation to Rick Solomon, as great a friend as a person could ever have.

And sincere thanks to Matt Bialer, Wendy Finerman, Dennis Gilbert, Gary Greengrass, Barry Halper, Dr. Sherwin Harris, Paula Kaplan, Susanna Lanner, Anita Lovely, Desiree Pilachowski, Judge Victor Reichman, Mitch Rose, Jeff Sanders, Jack Smalling, Jr., Robert Stricker, and Eric Vohn.

For their help with the photographs, my thanks to Mary Brace at Brace Photo, W. C. Burdick at the National Baseball Hall of Fame, Jennifer Clapp at UPI/Corbis-Bettman Archives, Jorge Jaramillo at AP Photo, and Kirk Kandle.

Thank you also to my wonderful parents, Joan and Steve Swirsky; my brother, David; my sister, Karen; and my Grandma Mimi Finkle. I want to further acknowledge my Grandpere Joel Finkle; his wife, Maria; my late grandparents, Ruth and Barney Swirsky; and Ida Sendroff, my late Godmother.

This project would not have been as much fun if I had not been able to share my "Baseball Letters" with many of my old friends: Mark Gimpel, Billy Spitalnick, Herb Hollander, Jimmy Berlstein, Eddie Chacon, and Tom Schiff.

I would also like to acknowledge great mentors and friends who are no longer here: Ed Amrhein, Peter Allen, and especially Irwin Schuster.

Finally, to all of the baseball players who have made so many people happy over the years—Thank you!

Photography Credits

Sandy Amoros (pp. 46–47); Tony Conigliaro (p. 67); Joe DiMaggio (pp. 80–81); Dwight D. Eisenhower (pp. 62–63); Mickey Mantle (p. 34); Babe Ruth (pp. 72–73); Norm Sherry (p. 113)—AP/Wide World Photo

Richie Ashburn (p. 120); Elden Auker (p. 57); Ken Brett with George Brett (p. 38); George Cisar (p. 134); Bobby Doerr (p. 156); Bob Feller with Johnny Rigney (p. 122); Rick Ferrell and Wes Ferrell (p. 41); Al Gionfriddo (p. 28); Buddy Hassett (p. 96); Jim Kaat (p. 78); Al Kaline (p. 88); Harmon Killebrew (p. 22); Clem Labine (p. 140); Hobie Landrith (p. 98); Leo Nonnenkamp (p. 124); Brooks Robinson (p. 92); Al Rosen (p. 58); Bobby Shantz (p. 127); Art Smith (p. 106); Duke Snider (p. 44); Bobby Thomson (p. 30)—George Brace

Bleacher fans (pp. 60–61); Frenchy Bordagaray with Pepper Martin's Mudcat Band (p. 138); Dolph Camilli (pp. 26–27); Woody English (p. 2); Joe Ginsberg (p. 100); Hank Greenberg (p. 57); Don Gutteridge (p. 158); Joe Hauser (p. 75); Solly Hemus with Stan Musial (p. 148); Ferguson Jenkins (p. 110); Johnny Pesky (p. 50); Dusty Rhodes (p. 145); waving fans (p. 180); Ted Williams (p. 14); Ted Williams with Bill Terry, Rogers Hornsby, and George Sisler (pp. 16–17); Jimmy Wynn (p. 109) —National Baseball Library and Archive, Cooperstown, New York

Hank Aaron (p. 43); Candlestick Park (p. 160); Sal Durante and Roger Maris (p. 52); Ebbets Field (p. ii); Eddie Gaedel (pp. 8–9); Monte Irvin with Willie Mays (p. 116); Jerry Koosman, Jerry Grote, and Ed Charles (#5) (p. 104); Don Larsen (p. 6); Fred Lynn (p. 102); Tim McClelland, George Brett, and Dick Howser (p. 37); Marty Marion and Enos Slaughter (p. 95); Johnny Podres and Roy Campanella (pp. 48–49); Cal Ripken, Jr., and Cal Ripken, Sr. (p. 4); Jackie Robinson (p. 11); Billy Rogell and Dizzy Dean (p. 129); Pete Rose, Johnny Bench, Joe Morgan, Tony Perez, and Davy Concepcion (p. 133); Joe Rudi (p. 142); Yankee Stadium (p. xii)—UPI/Corbis-Bettmann Archives

Autographed baseballs (p. 82)—Christian Davies

"The Called Shot" (p. 2, top)—Matt Kandle, Sr., © 1992 Kirk Kandle

Ron Cey with Bill Russell, Davey Lopes, and Steve Garvey (p. 130)—*The Sporting News*

Bill Buckner (p. 18); Paul Hopkins (p. 71); Whitey Lockman (p. 149)—courtesy of the author

About the Author

Seth Swirsky grew up in Great Neck, New York, where he struggled over the choice of emulating either Carl Yastrzemski or Paul McCartney. After being graduated from Dartmouth College, he opted for the latter, and became a songwriter with Chappell Music. His songs have been recorded by such artists as Celine Dion, Tina Turner, Air Supply, and Michael McDonald, among others. In 1987 and 1988, "Tell It To My Heart" and "Prove Your Love," both sung by Taylor Dayne, were worldwide Top Ten hits. Swirsky's "Love Is A Beautiful Thing," sung by Al Green, was featured in the 1996 movie *The Pallbearer.* Swirsky is an avid collector of baseball memorabilia and a lifelong New York Mets fan. He and his wife, Jody Gerson, live in Los Angeles with their two-year-old son, Julian.

Bleacher fans wait in the rain for Yankee Stadium to open for the '55 World Series.